D0818954

Public Church

OTHER LUTHERAN VOICES TITLES

See www.lutheranvoices.com

Public Church
For the Life of the World

Cynthia D. Moe-Lobeda

Augsburg Fortress

Minneapolis

PUBLIC CHURCH
For the Life of the World

Copyright © 2004 Augsburg Fortress. All rights reserved. Except for brief quotations in critical articles or reviews, no part of this book may be reproduced without prior written permission from the publisher. Write to: Permissions, Augsburg Fortress, Box 1209, Minneapolis,
MN 55440.

Large-quantity purchases or custom editions of these books are available at a discount from
the publisher. For more information, contact the sales department at Augsburg Fortress,
Publishers, 1-800-328-4648, or write to: Sales Director, Augsburg Fortress, Publishers, P.O.
Box 1209, Minneapolis, MN 55440-1209.

Direct Scripture quotations are from New Revised Standard Version Bible, copyright © 1989
Division of Christian Education of the National Council of the Churches of Christ in the
United States of America. Used by permission.

Editor: Scott Tunseth

Cover design: © Koechel Peterson and Associates, Inc., Minneapolis, MN
        www.koechelpeterson.com

Cover photo: © Koechel Peterson and Associates, Inc., Minneapolis, MN

ISBN 0-8066-4987-9

The paper used in this publication meets the minimum requirements of American
National Standard for Information Sciences—Permanence of Paper for Printed Library
Materials, ANSI Z329.48-1984.

Manufactured in the U.S.A.

08   07   06   05   04   1   2   3   4   5   6   7   8   9   10

This book is dedicated to Ron for sharing a lifetime of deepening and mysterious love with me, and to Leif and Gabriel, for being who they are and for bringing indescribable joy into my life. And it is dedicated to Rosemary, truly a wise woman and bearer of God's Spirit.

Contents

Preface and Acknowledgments

There is a kind of audacity in doing theology, in setting words and reason to the unfathomable yet intimate mystery that we call God. How are we to think and speak of what it means to live as a people claimed by one who is boundless love for this good earth and its creatures, we human ones included? We live in a time of unprecedented dangers and possibilities. At this moment in history, as this church seeks to discern the shape of faithful witness, may we be ever mindful that our knowing is limited, and God's trustworthiness is not. May we always trust that the embrace of God's healing and liberating love extends further and deeper than we can imagine.

We live within a "cloud of witnesses" throughout the ages who have struggled faithfully and faultily to discern what it means to be a people of the God revealed in Jesus Christ and known through the Spirit, what it means, that is, to be church in each time and place. I love to envision this church today encircled by that motley throng. I believe that their witness is not bound by time. They speak wisdom to us yet today, both through their mistakes and their faithfulness, if we listen both appreciatively and critically. As this church continues to discern its public vocation in our time, may we learn from the profound faithfulness and the terrible errors of our faith forebears.

Books have many beginning points. Tracing them is, perhaps, like hiking back up to the headwaters of a river looking for the many streams that trickle together to make it. This book is not mine alone. It began not as a book but as an invitation from Mark Hanson, the Presiding Bishop of the Evangelical Lutheran Church in America, to serve as theological consultant to an inquiry by the ELCA into the public vocation of this church in these times. That initiative had grown out of the conversations and activities of numerous groups within the church. All were seeking to better understand the contours of faithful witness in the complex and tumultuous world in which God has called us together and sent us forth, not only as individuals but as a people, "to proclaim the good news of God in Christ through word and deed, to serve all people following the example of our

Lord Jesus Christ, and to strive for justice and peace in all the earth." This inquiry into the church's public vocation engaged leadership of the ELCA in its many expressions: congregations, seminary and church college presidents and faculty, parish pastors, synodical bishops, staff of the churchwide office, leaders of social ministry networks affiliated with the ELCA and of its advocacy and community organizing efforts, and others. One of my roles as theological consultant was to write an extensive paper that would inform the process by articulating theological foundations, unfolding dimensions, and raising key questions about the ELCA's role in the public life of communities, the nation, and the world at this time in history. That paper generated widespread interest and appreciation. Requests for it lead to its development into a book for publication. May it continue to spur spirited questioning, fruitful deliberation, passionate conversation, and daring faithful action.

Through this rich process, the book benefited from the initiative and wisdom of many dedicated and creative members of this church. In particular, I am indebted to Bishop Mark Hanson for his theological acumen, willingness to risk, and splendid mix of piety and prophecy, and to Rebecca Larson for her sharp intellect, faithful vision, and strength. The inquiry into "public church" has enabled me to know many people who work in the ELCA's church-wide offices in Chicago. I stand in awe of their commitment, creativity, raw tenacity, intelligence, ability to laugh and weep, and commitment to serve God through the church. To them, I offer my respect and gratitude. To Anne-Marie Bogdan, I extend, in addition, my deep regard for her splendid initial editing of the paper that became this book.

This book has been informed too by recent substantive work with the Lutheran World Federation, the World Council of Churches, and the World Alliance of Reformed Churches. It has been a great privilege to work with and learn from theologians of Latin America, Africa, Asia, and Europe. Their voices have been present with me in the crafting of this work. Written about the public witness of church in a nation with tremendous power in the global public, this book would not have integrity had I not drawn upon the wisdom and experience of sisters and brothers from other lands. I thank Karen Bloomquist for having first invited me into these circles.

At Augsburg Fortress Publishers, I thank Scott Tunseth for his perseverance, calm, wisdom, and steady support; Michael West for having initially risked welcoming me as an author with Fortress Press and for his sagacity and intellectual agility in the world of theological publishing; Beth Lewis for her delightful enthusiasm for this project; Bob Todd for his dedication and reliability; James Korsmo for the demanding work of proofreading; and all others who have enabled this project to go forward, but whose names I do not know.

I thank the misty grey dawns of the Pacific Northwest for inspiration and for daily opening my heart to the Spirit. The book was written in large part in two Seattle coffee shops. I am indebted to the good and gracious people who work at Greenwood Tullys and Diva Espresso for their smiles, laughter, encouragement, and unending refills of delicious decaf!

To precious friends in Seattle and afar, I am ever grateful for feeding my soul with their friendship. My colleagues, teachers, and mentors in Christian ethics and other fields of theological studies, I thank for their continued intellectual generosity, formative influence, and investment in my work. Without them, I think I could not think well! I only hope that I may honor them by returning the same quality of support to them and to others. My students, I thank for their questions and spirit, and for giving me the deep joy of working with them.

Finally, but most of all, I thank the three splendid human beings with whom I am blessed to share life and home: my two utterly wonderful sons, Leif and Gabriel, and the love of my life, Ron. You have put up with my long hours of labor over this book, and have nurtured me when the going was rough. You recall me to gratitude and awe for the beauty of life and the presence of God's Spirit . . . for I see them in you.

Introduction

"You have made public profession of your faith. Do you intend to continue in the covenant God made with you in Holy Baptism:
> *to live among God's faithful people,*
> *to hear the Word of God and share in the Lord's supper,*
> *to proclaim the good news of God in Christ through word and deed,*
> *to serve all people, following the example of our Lord Jesus,*
> *to strive for justice and peace in all the earth?"*
"I do, and I ask God to help and guide me."
> ⟫Lutheran Book of Worship[1]

"Consistent with the faith and practice of the Evangelical Lutheran Church in America, every ordained minister shall: . . . conduct public worship . . . speak publicly to the world in solidarity with the poor and oppressed, calling for justice and proclaiming God's love for the world."
> ⟫Constitutions, Bylaws, and Continuing Resolutions of the
> Evangelical Lutheran Church in America[2]

"Proclamation of the Word includes the public reading of Scripture, preaching, teaching, the celebration of the sacraments, confession and absolution, music, arts, prayers, Christian witness, and service."
> ⟫"The Use of the Means of Grace: A Statement on the Practice of
> Word and Sacrament"[3]

"Sing with all the people of God, and join in the hymn of all creation."
> ⟫Lutheran Book of Worship[4]

In baptismal vows and prayers, teachings, constitution, liturgy, order of ordination, and confessional documents, the Evangelical Lutheran Church in America (ELCA) professes to be a public church and a church constituted by God for a public vocation. What, then, does this mean for us—the ELCA—and our role in public life today? The response is at once breathtakingly simple and confoundingly complex, as is the life of faith itself.

The shape of life as public church in public life is determined by whose we are, by what God calls and sends us to do, and by having been made—by God—into an assembly of believers. In Baptism, God claims us as God's own, gives us our vocation, and weaves us into an assembly, the church, so "that we may" fulfill that calling[5]. This book is fashioned around a journey through the marks of the baptized, as identified in the Affirmation of Baptism (cited in the opening quote above).

This book moves through five chapters, each building on the previous. The first chapter unfolds a few guidelines for faithful response to the question of what it means to be public church, and then untangles implications of "public," especially when connected with "church." The second explores what this public church and its public vocation are, in light of the covenant God makes with us in Holy Baptism. The third uncovers key obstacles deterring this church from our public vocation.[6] The fourth chapter reflects on God's gift of power to be who we are as public church, to live our public vocation. Together, these four parts invite one to understand this church to be a people of the incarnation *as a way of living* in and for the world today. The fifth and final chapter begins to explore what that "way of living" looks like for the ELCA at the dawn of the 21st century.

The aim throughout is to point in fruitful directions, raise questions, and uncover Lutheran theological resources that may serve this church in its commitment to "step forward as a public church that witnesses boldly to God's love for all that God has created."[7]

1

Starting Points

Guidelines for Faithful and Fruitful Response

The question of the church's role in public life is an enduring one. Christians have grappled with it for two millennia. It was, in fact, a central point of difference among Christian communities of the first two centuries, the initial formative era of Christian morality.[1]

> *"Morality" and "ethics" often are used synonymously. While this is understandable—"ethics" comes from the Greek, and "morality" comes from the word used by Cicero to translate the Greek to Latin—there is an important distinction. Morality is a dimension of life—not a separate pursuit, but a dimension of any pursuit. It is the dimension that asks, consciously or not, whether a way of doing or being is good, right, and fitting in a given circumstance. Moral consciousness is awareness of the distinction between "what is" and "what ought and could be." Ethics refers to the disciplined inquiry into morality. One could say ethics is the art-science of bringing self-consciousness, method, intentionality, and sensitivity to the tasks of (1) discerning what is good and right for any given situation and context, (2) finding the moral-spiritual power to act on that discernment, and (3) discovering what forms individuals and society toward the good and what malforms them away from it. This book will use the two terms—morality and ethics—as distinguished here.*

A response usually grows from the interplay between a particular historical context and traditional faith claims, especially regarding the being and doing of the church. How the church has understood its identity and purpose profoundly impacts its public life both internally and in relationship to the world beyond the boundaries of the church. Just when we get settled in an understanding of "church" and its role in public life, we may be propelled to re-ask the question or reinterpret our understanding. The motivating force may be a new era in human history, a crisis in the church or in the broader society, or the Spirit's insistent prodding.

The church is, like other manifestations of the presence of God, mystery. Mysteries of God are not hidden realities, but realities being revealed by God in and through our experience by the power of Christ and the Holy Spirit. We are called to know such realities ever more fully, but not completely, in human lifetimes. We (and here I mean the ELCA) are yet unfolding our understanding of the mystery of being church.

Given the lifetimes already spent probing questions of the church's public vocation, and given the variety of faithful and prudent responses, the people engaging this inquiry today might be wise to

1. Recall the Lutheran insistence that ambiguity and paradox are unavoidable, and thus avoid any claim to know absolutely the correct Christian answer to the questions, or even the correct Lutheran-Christian answer for our time and place. Perhaps it would be wiser, in our conclusions, not to prescribe and prohibit absolutely, but rather to offer overall directions and parameters, held within the claim that these will re-form as we—by the Spirit's power—mature in being God's "rusty tools,"[2] and as the Word of God continues "to change and renew the world" (Luther's words).[3]

2. Take seriously a prior question, the question of method: how are we as a church to arrive at normative responses to the question, "What is the role of the ELCA in public life?" What sources guide responses to that question, and how do those sources work together? They include, for example, the Lutheran Confessions, the writings of Luther, subsequent Lutheran teachings and theological reflections, the input of the Lutheran communion worldwide, and the experience of ecumenical brothers and sisters and the interfaith community. By what methods might the ELCA draw most fruitfully upon these sources?

3. Acknowledge the multiple organizing principles for this discussion offered by the rich, lively, and living Lutheran theological heritage.
4. Remember that we stand in good company among a cloud of witnesses throughout the ages, seeking in faith to understand what it means to be church today. How, as church, are we to participate in God's mission in and for the world?
5. Recognize that this church has engaged the question valiantly. In doing so we build on a rich history of lived faith and theological inquiry.
6. Carry forth our heritage by reflecting on it trustingly, critically, and constructively.
7. Bear in mind that being who God has made us in Christ, as a public church, may pose difficulties and dangers on a practical level. In order to avoid them, we may be tempted to abridge our understanding of the church's public vocation (more on this later). Note here simply that resisting this temptation requires acknowledging the problems and risks entailed in being a public church, rather than trying to pretend they do not exist.

The fifth, sixth, and third of these guidelines warrant further attention.

A Rich History
Lutherans have a long and rich history of engagement in public life for the sake of the world, and an equally rich theological tradition undergirds this legacy. This tradition begins with Luther's insistence that *because* we are made righteous before God by grace though Christ, we are freed from orienting our lives around the quest for our own salvation. We are freed *for* orienting life around praise and thanksgiving to God, and around active love for neighbor. The Augsburg Confession and other confessional documents elaborate the implications of that foundational faith claim. It sent earthquakes through the social world of Luther's day, disrupting long-standing economic and cultural assumptions. This dramatic reorientation of life gives overall shape to the church's public vocation today.

Lutheran tradition, building on Luther and the Confessions throughout the subsequent five centuries, has developed distinct theological guideposts for this church's witness. These include

- an absolute assurance that human works are in no way salvific;
- a paradoxical *simul justus et peccator* ("simultaneously righteous and sinner") anthropology;
- a "now . . . not yet" eschatology;[4]
- a distinction between the reign of God and any humanly constructed system;
- the celebration of reason, except for the purpose of knowing *who* God is and that God is "for us" (*pro nobis*);
- acknowledgment of the pervasive presence of sin in human life, of ambiguity and complexity in morality, of the hiddenness of God's works in the form of their opposite as demonstrated most fully in the cross, and of the human proclivity to believe we can define and control God; and
- an affirmation of the created goodness of creation, the vocation of all believers, and experience as central in theology.

Lutherans have interpreted these themes variously, and have debated and contested them and their implications for public witness. At their best, these lively conversations have nourished faithful public witness. This book neither enters nor summarizes those debates. Rather, it assumes these themes as valuable guideposts, draws upon them, and builds (with the gratitude of the author) on the work of countless others who point to the contributions and limitations of these themes in various contexts.

A Triple Hermeneutic

Lutheran theological heritage, while rich and faithful, is simultaneously flawed. This should come as no surprise to a church deeply cognizant of the *simul* nature of human existence in God. While at times Lutheran theological themes have served the church's public witness, in other instances they have obstructed it. An integral task of theology is the critical task. This particular faith tradition, as all ecclesial traditions, is obligated to critical self-awareness regarding ways in which it has, even with the best of intentions, obscured the gospel. At the cusp of the new century, seeking guidance for our life as public church, we plumb the depths of the Lutheran theological heritage with a triple hermeneutic.

Through a *hermeneutic of trust,* we seek in our heritage the song of the living God, trusting that traditional themes bear profound wisdom for today, and trusting too that deep and powerful Lutheran theological resources for this day remain yet untapped. Through a *hermeneutic of suspicion,* in dialogue within this church and with others ecumenically and globally, we are alert for where the founding teachings and their interpreters may obscure or distort the voice of God. A *constructive hermeneutic* bids us build upon both the faithfulness and the mistakes of our faith forebears. These three approaches are interdependent and are integral to faithful theological inquiry. Held together, they are fertile terrain. Entering it thoroughly is, of course, beyond the scope of a single undertaking. In this one, I attempt to honor all three interpretive lenses, at least illustratively. I draw upon traditional themes, suggest a few fault lines in them, and probe less familiar Lutheran theological gems that offer wisdom for the ELCA as it unfolds its vocation in public life. In particular, I draw upon Martin Luther, convinced that he offers splendid resources for the life of this public church today.

Multiple Theological Entry Points
One may organize a Lutheran ethic or theology of "public church in public life" around any of three or four different legitimate centerpieces. Luther certainly did so, as have others. Historically, Lutherans have framed discussions of the church in public life around the two-fold rule of God, commonly referred to as "two kingdoms." It is a rich resource—especially in 20th-century interpretations seeking to undo the dualism that characterized the theme in the 19th century—and could frame the discussion at hand fruitfully. However, I have chosen to relocate the discussion of church in public life in the incarnation of Christ as seen in cross, resurrection, and living presence.

I have three reasons for this decision. First, discussions of public witness centered around "two kingdoms" thought almost invariably becomes reduced to the relationship of church to state, thus obscuring other issues of church in public life (such as the church's relationship to economy, to civil society, and to cultural dimensions such as race/ethnicity and gender).[5] Second, I have a passionate sense that Lutheran theology bears additional theological riches for our day, but I am concerned that this church may fail to use its gifts for the sake of the world and fail to be Lutheran in the footsteps of Luther and the other confessors, if we do not delve into those resources. They are overlooked or obscured when we remain bound primarily to the categories in which we most frequently have discussed the church in public life. Some of these resources lie in Luther's sense of the living Word of God permeating and changing all of life through Christ crucified and risen and through the Holy Spirit. It is a profound theology of the cross located in a theology of the incarnation, and expressed in Luther's sermons, treatises, and biblical commentary.

Third, "two kingdoms" theology has contested meanings and implications for public life. The teaching has been interpreted differently throughout history, and the interpretations are consequential. The concepts involved are so multifaceted and disputed that the teaching becomes difficult to use with integrity without first entering those disputes (so doing would require a separate book). They concern Luther's intentions in identifying "two kingdoms" and "two governances/regiments," the theological significance of his shift from distinguishing between "kingdoms" (*Reiche*) and "governance" (*Regimente*) to—after AD 1523—using them interchangeably, and the various dialectical relationships to which these terms refer in "Temporal Authority" and elsewhere. Furthermore, it is not simple to distinguish between what Luther meant and what later Lutheran theologians have meant by the "two kingdoms," or to assess the extent to which interpretations represent Luther's actual teachings.[6] Lutherans go on to debate the doctrine's historical effects on political consciousness and actions, the validity of criticism that the doctrine has led to moral quietism and dualism—or even that it inevitably does—and whether or not this teaching can be considered "a definable doctrine at all."[7] Becoming embroiled in studying and reflecting on these debates would distract from the task at hand. To that task we proceed, after a brief foray into the meanings and import of "public."

The Meaning of "Public"

"Public" is a theologically and morally rich concept vibrant with significance for the church. The term's connotations and denotations are varied, shifting, and contested. Here I do not enter the theoretical debates regarding "public." Rather, my intent is first to note problematic connotations of the term, so that this church might avoid those problems. Secondly, I will illumine the particular import of *public* identity and vocation for the church in North America in an age of privitization.

A Contested Term

"Public" appears as both adjective and noun in documents of the ELCA, as in the broader public discourse.[8] We will consider both uses. As an adjective, "public" frequently is contrasted, misleadingly, with "personal": some aspects of life are personal and others are public. The two are disassociated, and what is personal is understood as *not* public and as not having public impact. Accordingly, for example, a "personal relationship with God" would be considered inconsequential for public life, needs, or social structures. The common practice of contrasting public to personal is a misuse of both terms. More accurately, "public" ought be juxtaposed not with "personal" but with "private." What is public may be very personal, but not necessarily private. This coheres with the Lutheran affirmation that worship is inherently public and personal.

While a distinction between private and public is important, many feminist theorists critique the use of that distinction in liberal political theory. Liberalism divided society into a public sphere of economics and politics, and a private sphere of domestic life. Associated with the latter were family and household care, sexuality, moral formation, feelings, and women's lives. Here the Christian moral norm of Christ-like love pertained, its highest form being self-sacrificial love. The public sphere was the world of government and business, morally neutral economic theory, rationality, and men. As theorized by Reinhold Niebuhr, this was a world of competing interests striving for power. In this sphere, the norm of self-sacrificing love was irrelevant, at best an "impossible possibility." The norm of justice—understood as a relatively equitable balance of power between competing interests—took the place of love. The two spheres were discrete. Feminist political theorists, while upholding a distinction between public and private, refute the way that liberal theory constructed that separation, arguing that it served the interests of men and of the reigning economic order. The public/private split rendered self-sacrifice normative for women but not for men, confined the work of women to home and family, and freed the economic and political worlds from any accountability to the Christian norm of neighbor-love. In addition, the split protected freedom in the private sphere as freedom from public regulation or intervention. Thus, domestic violence against women was long held as a private matter, exempt from public legal censure.

Finally, in some discourse, "public" is understood as referencing the governmental sector of society, in contrast to business and civil society. As Ronald Thiemann notes, "This severely truncates the sphere of the *res publica,* the sphere which in classical political theory refers to . . . society as a whole."[9] Were this connotation assumed, the church's public witness would be limited to the relationship of church to government.

Informed by these insights, as we unfold an understanding of "public" church in public life, let us juxtapose "public" to "private," rather than to "personal." And let us reconceptualize both "public" and "private" to break with the aforementioned dualistic and constraining constructions. A primary meaning of "public" as an adjective is "open and accessible" to all.[10] Theologically, "open and accessible to all" is joined by "for the sake of all." Describing church or worship as "public" declares that the church and its worship are decidedly not "private." They are open and accessible to all and are for the sake of the world, rather than being open to a select few and for the sake of that select few. The church is not just a group of people gathered for its own sake behind closed doors.

As a noun, "public" is controversial around similar lines, and three additional issues appear. Liberal theory tends to presuppose a singular public, that, while composed of many different kinds of people, is served by one common good and may be spoken for as a whole. Unquestioning acceptance of a *singular* public with a singular common good may become a "veneer for the legitimation of elite interests,"[11] excluding the perspectives and interests of the less powerful. In a society offering "unequal access to the common good and the effective forging of it,"[12] a presupposed singular public and singular common good may perpetuate that inequality by obscuring it. For this reason, wherever possible, I will use the term "good of all" or "widespread good" instead of "common good."

Second, "public"—anthropocentrically conceived—tends to exclude all but human participants in the earth community. Yet developments of the last four decades in theology, biological and earth sciences, and cosmology point to the amazing interconnectedness of Earth's life forms, suggesting that the scope of the public ought to extend beyond the human. Finally, some theologians have assumed that "public"—used as a noun—is autonomous from church.[13] The problem here is failure to recognize that, throughout history, the boundaries between the two are porous.

To avoid these problems, let us assume that "public" as noun will imply difference and power differentials, have multiple scopes (that is, neighborhood, locality, nation, world community, community of life), and not be autonomous from church. "Public" refers to the domain of human activity that is not simply private, individual, or for "members only," but is focused on the good of all. For the purpose at hand, public is the "arena of the church's vocation,"[14] the world "for the sake of" which this church is "claimed, gathered, and sent,"[15] and of which it is a part. The public may extend to the vast interrelated household of God's creation. While the overall role of the public church in public life does not change, how that role plays out is contextual, depending upon the circumstances of the "public" and of the church in any given situation. Participating in God's mission assumes differing modes in different dimensions of public, hinging, in part, on where we as church stand in relationship to various power structures.

These controversies around "public" may serve this church well, as we mature in our life as public church in public life. They caution against misuses of the term, and push us to expand and complexify our understanding of the "public" and of the public church's role in public life. Awareness of the provocative theorizing around "public" may aid this church in continuing to uncover and unfold distinctively Lutheran theological contributions regarding the public church. Insights into "public" might, for example, open new paths in the lively discussion within the Lutheran community worldwide concerning the public significance of justification.

Public amidst Private

Increasingly in the last three decades, the "privatization" of goods, services, and knowledge previously considered public has emerged as a defining characteristic of the cultural, political, and economic ethos. Privatization in the current era gives to companies or individuals, often not accountable to the communities impacted, ownership of basic goods; of services such as water, electricity, health care, and education; and of intellectual property in the form of patents. (For goods and services previously not considered marketable in either a private or a public sense, a first step in privatization may be "commodification." This refers to giving something a monetary value and placing it on the market.)[16] This trend spans the globe and has far-reaching and profound moral implications. It helps to determine who will have and who will not have what is needed for life with dignity, and to shape the terms of humankind's relationship to our planetary home.

Here is not the place to analyze the economic theory undergirding this trend, or to assess the validity of the theory's various components.[17] Suffice it here to flag concerns that the elevation of the "private" ought to raise for a cloud of witnesses commanded, taught, and empowered by God to "love thy neighbor as thyself." Elevation of the "private" may draw attention away from the dignity and needs of those who are impoverished or otherwise vulnerable, and while clouding our vision for seeing all of life through the lens of God's love for this world. The purpose in noting these concerns is to highlight the moral and theological import of a church confessing and professing to be *public* rather than private, especially in the context of a widespread race toward privatization.

Consider five particular concerns. First, when basic goods required for survival are commodified and privatized, what happens to people who do not have the money to purchase them on the open market? What happens to society when increasing numbers of people are debilitated by efforts to live without their basic needs being met?[18]

Second are the moral implications of commodifying and privatizing human genetic materials. Are the human rights of aboriginal people betrayed when a global corporation gains exclusive legal right to their human genetic material? What happens to cancer research and the cost of treatment when a single private enterprise gains exclusive right to particular genetic resources that may give rise to a cure or a powerful treatment?

The United Nations Human Development Programme and a broad spectrum of international Non-Governmental Organizations (NGO's) articulate another concern related to the privatization of knowledge. New and tighter patent laws on intellectual property are being generated by the World Trade Organization. At the same time, increasing percentages of research funding are going to private corporations. "This trend has been particularly strong in agriculture and biotechnology . . . [As a result,] the best of the new technologies are priced for those who can pay."[19] Most troubling has been the negative impact on the availability of low cost medication for AIDS in Africa, and on subsistence farmers. What is the fate, for example, of subsistence farmers in India when the seed strain that has enabled their lives for generations past is bought up by a large company, slightly modified genetically, patented, and then usable by its original farmers only when purchased by them? What becomes of the farm families and communities who no longer may continue to plant the farm-saved seed that is a mainstay of their diet and their barter economy?

The privatization of faith or of spirituality presents a fourth concern. The Christian tradition, like the other two shared Abrahamic faiths, cannot conceive of privatized faith. Reborn into the life of Christ, Christians become part of a cloud of witnesses, an assembly of the faithful, utterly dependent upon each other as the "body" through which the living Christ speaks and acts. According to the covenant God makes with us in Baptism, we are called to hear and proclaim the Word of God, share in the sacraments, bear one another's burdens, and "love neighbor as self." These are integral dimensions of our faith, our spirituality, our morality. More on this striking gift of interdependence later. Here, the point is to question the current and widespread trend toward privatized "spirituality" or privatized faith.

Finally, many argue that the citizenship of the U.S. on the whole, is increasingly oriented more around the private good (the good of me and those close to me) than the public good.[20] The morality of individual lives garners more serious scrutiny than the moral condition of society. Said differently, the turn is toward a "privatized view of the good life," and toward privatized morality itself.[21] This "eclipse of the common good" betrays understandings of morality stemming from Aristotle and from commonly accepted historical Christian teaching.[22] To secure the good for the people in common, Aristotle asserts, "is nobler and more divine" than to attain it for oneself. "One of Aristotle's most significant contributions," notes Jesuit ethicist David Hollenbach, "was that a good life is oriented to goods shared with others—the common good of the larger society . . ."[23]

Biblically and theologically considered, concern for the public good is integral to life as people of God, and is positively valued. The biblical witness, as I understand it, holds that God created humans for community on many levels, from intimate circles to societies, and that communities—be they the ancient Hebrews or contemporary societies—are to shape ways of life together (public life) that praise God by actively serving the widespread good. People are to collaborate publicly to shape those ways of life in common. Public life, in service of the public good, is a reflection of our createdness as beings-in-relationship[24] who are called to witness to God's love for this beautiful and broken world.

Amidst this turn to the private, the church of God is called to the *missio dei*, a public vocation for the sake of God's creation, the vast public. The inherently public character and vocation of the people gathered and sent in the name of Christ shine as "evangelical defiance" to the privatization of life. Irenaeus of Lyon, leader of a second-century martyred community in what is now France, described the Holy Spirit as the "dew of God . . . diffused throughout all the Earth."[25] It is hard to imagine anything more public than this dew, the Spirit of God, and the church moistened by it and sent throughout all the world.

Questions for Reflection

1. At the outset of this study, describe your understanding of what it means to be "church." What do you understand to be the church's vocation in public life? Do you see any reasons to revisit those understandings?

2. Re-read the fourth of the "guidelines for faithful and fruitful response." What people or communities do you see as part of that "cloud of witnesses" throughout the ages . . . seeking to understand what it means to be church in and for the world? What can be learned from faithful witnesses who have gone before us?

3. Page 4 identifies a number of characteristically Lutheran theological themes that are relevant to the church's public witness. Chose two or three of them. In what ways have you seen or experienced these themes helping to shape the faithful public witness of this church? In what ways have you seen or experienced the themes impeding faithful public witness?

4. In what ways have you experienced the "privatization" of goods, services, experiences, knowledge, genetic material, faith and spirituality, or views of the good life? Does a trend toward privatization of life raise flags for you as a follower of Jesus Christ? Why or why not?

2

Being Public Church
in Public Life

What is this public church, its vocation, and the implications of these for the church's role in public life? The Evangelical Lutheran Church in America is blessed with theologically rich and solid responses to this question.[1] According to the ELCA constitution, "The church is a people created by God in Christ,[2] empowered by the Holy Spirit, called and sent to bear witness to God's creative, redeeming, and sanctifying activity in the world . . . to participate in God's mission . . ."[3] This church "confesses" that it is created and sustained by God "for God's mission in the world."[4]

The constitution goes on to affirm what this church "shall" do "to participate in God's mission."[5] The list is an eloquent elaboration of our baptismal vows. This is fitting, for it is in Baptism that "by water and the Holy Spirit we are made members of the church."[6]

According to these commonly held affirmations, the church is an assembly of baptized believers sharing Word and Supper, created and claimed by God in Christ, and given power by the Holy Spirit in order to worship God and to proclaim and participate in what God is doing in the world. We refer to this work of God as "God's mission in the world." We are part of the broader church, the cloud of witnesses throughout the ages claimed, gathered, and sent by God's grace to give thanks for that work of God, witness to it, and give it social form.

Let us assume that these affirmations are solid, are worth living into. Let us assume further that the current times propel us to explore anew the very mysteries that these affirmations express. What do they mean for who we are and how we are to live as public church and church in public life, in the Lutheran tradition, in this place now and for the foreseeable future?

A clue of infinite worth is in God's covenant made with us in Baptism. Our affirmation of intent to live in that covenant sketches the life of the public church. Baptized members are called and committed—through the covenant made by God in Baptism—"to hear God's Word and share in God's Supper;" "to proclaim the good news of God in Christ through word and deed;" "to serve all people, following the example of our Lord Jesus;" "to strive for justice and peace in all the earth;" and "to live among God's faithful people."[7] This chapter considers what this church and its vocation are and what these mean for our life in public today in light of each of the five marks of the baptized.

"To Hear the Word of God and Share in the Lord's Supper"

The public church is an assembly of baptized believers that

- receives and is being changed and renewed by the living Christ in the preached Word;
- receives, remembers, and is being changed and renewed by the living Christ in the Eucharist; and
- thanks God, in words and deeds, for God's love for all of creation.

The church gathers the people, receives the Word, breaks the bread, gives thanks, and sends the people forth to serve God. Word and Supper throw those who receive them into public matters of life and death, for in the hearing and the tasting we receive Christ. We receive one who was killed publicly for his unwavering dedication to the reign of God, proclaimed in word and deed. The consequences for how we live in the world are monumental, stunning. They would be frightening were they not born of grace, grace both as forgiveness for our shortcomings and as the power and presence of God working in and among us.

The earliest Christians called themselves *ekklesia*, assembly. They were and we are the assembly gathered by the power of the Spirit around and into the presence of the living Christ. That Christ-presence is uniquely present in Word and Sacrament. Christ is received. The people gathered are made new, "as if they were being awakened from sleep, born anew to life, raised from the dead."[8] The assembled hear God's truth and take it into their body and bodies. The people gathered around Jesus Christ remember who they are. They recall the new vision they have been given for the world and of the world through the lens of God's love for it. They remember their vocation. By the power of the Spirit, they witness to God's saving love in the everyday practices of life. The people publicly practice the new vision. The Word flows out of the public assembly into the broader public. Living as body of Christ for the healing of the world—serving God's mission in the world—is the "liturgy after the liturgy."

"The Word of God, wherever it comes, comes to change and renew the world."[9] Lutherans confess the Word of God to be, first and foremost, Christ become human, crucified, risen, and living. The creating, saving, sustaining presence of the living Christ changes everything. To proclaim or to receive the Word is to participate in God's work "to change and renew the world." The proclaimer and the hearer are "God's hands" in that work, God's "rusty tools."[10] In fact, according to Luther's almost quaint yet theoretically complex and loaded explanation, "[God] is able to help everyone . . . [H]e does not want to do it alone. He wants us to work with him . . . wants to work with us and through us."[11]

To "hear the Word" is not only a matter of the ears. It is a full-body event, engaging all the senses. The little children in my church hear the Word in drama. We see the Word in art. Our bodies feel it in the hands-on blessing of a healing service. Luther preaches that we are to "taste" the Word. "[T]hough it is a great and good gift even to have the Word thoroughly taught, [Paul] prays that the heart may taste the Word and that it may be effectual in the life."[12] Taste the Word? Perhaps Luther is provoking the people to know the word so fully, so deeply, that they taste it. How will this people, the ELCA, hear the Word so intimately that we taste it? What power for sharing and living the Word is evoked by hearing it that deeply?

The assembly shares God's Supper. Where the Eucharist is "properly" practiced, Luther teaches, it creates a community of people engaged in public life on behalf of the common good, especially the good of the vulnerable. The communing community is "changed" into a people who attend to human needs. They "help the poor, put up with sinners, care for the sorrowing, suffer with the suffering, intercede for others, defend the truth."[13] "Now there is no greater service of God [German *Gottesdienst*, worship] than Christian love which helps and serves the needy, as Christ himself will judge and testify at the Last Day, Matthew 25 [:31–46]."[14] The "liturgy after the liturgy" is the lived-out commitment to serve the public good, heeding particularly the needs of the impoverished.

In "The Blessed Sacrament of the Holy and True Body and Blood of Christ, and the Brotherhoods," Luther expresses the life-changing implications of the Eucharist:[15]

- "Christ has given his body for this purpose, that the one thing signified by the sacrament—the fellowship, the change wrought by love—may be put into practice."
- "The sacrament has no blessing and significance unless love grows daily and so changes a person that he is made one with the others."
- "Thus by means of this sacrament, all self-seeking love is rooted out and gives place to that which seeks the common good of all."
- "In times past this sacrament was so properly used, and the people were taught to understand this fellowship so well, that they even gathered food and material goods in the church, and then . . . distributed among those who were in need . . . [T]his has all disappeared, and now there remain only the many masses and the many who receive this sacrament without in the least understanding or practicing what it signifies . . . They will not help the poor, put up with sinners, care for the sorrowing, suffer with the suffering, intercede for others, defend the truth."

According to Luther, a fruit of the Eucharist is a community that tends to human needs, including material needs, and privileges the needs of the "vulnerable." This is a face of the church in public life.

Luther is not alone in the conviction that Word and Sacrament are life-altering, indeed world-altering. Since at least the time of Irenaeus of Lyons, the Eucharist has been known by some as a school for the senses and a school for Christian living. Liturgical theologian, Gordon Lathrop, revives this ancient wisdom, claiming that Christian liturgies shape and express cosmologies, and that these profoundly "orient" our relationships with self, others, and earth.[16] Word and Meal may shape the faithful toward justice-making, earth-honoring ways of living or may reinforce the opposite.

Of course, few things are more certain than that Christian assemblies—including the ELCA in its many expressions—are inevitably faulty and incomplete in being who God has made them. The brokenness of humanity extends to the faithful people of God. "Living among God's faithful people" is a constant reminder of the need for God's mercy and the certainty of it. Our life together expresses the *simul* reality in which our lives unfold: called to live as if the reign of God were "already" present, we live also knowing that it is "not yet." While God in Word and Sacrament turns the church toward the world to heal the world, we also are—in Luther's words—"selves turned in on self" (*se incurvatus in se*),[17] in both subtle and evident ways. As selves turned in on self, we must return and return and return to hear and taste the Word reminding us that God has come to be with us in our brokenness and to be in and among us.

Word and Eucharist are concrete and ancient Christian practices through which the living Christ comes to, into, and among the community of believers. In the midst of that community, Christ calls forth power for faith active in love, even if that love calls the faithful to swim upstream against torrential and dangerous social forces. To consider Word and Supper anew may be to uncover startling insights into our vocation as public church and into the roots of moral-spiritual power for living that vocation today. May this public church ever approach Word and Sacrament with gratitude, awe, and wonder, and with open hearts and minds and with keen questions. How and where do we hear the Word and celebrate the Sacrament of the Table in ways that open us ever more to receive "the change wrought by love [that it] may be put into practice"[18] in public life and to proclaim the good news of God in Jesus Christ? How does or could our public liturgy itself teach us that by means of this sacrament, "all self-seeking love is rooted out and gives place to that which seeks the common good of all"? How does or could sharing the Supper "form" the communing community to see God's justice and mercy at work in the world, and "conform" us to living it? Do Word and Meal "re-orient us" from lives "turned in on self" to lives lived toward the widespread good? These may be the compelling church-renewing liturgical, theological, and evangelical questions of our day.

Simply asking them in community with others and praying for guidance is potent. One of my most treasured roles in worship is to serve Communion. I have experienced as an incredible gift the privilege of saying, "This is the body of Christ given for you," as I look each person in the eye and speak her or his name. Only recently, while yearning for answers to questions like those above, did I learn that this practice, while infinitely rich, approaches only a portion of the eucharistic mystery. The "you" in this life-giving affirmation has a double meaning: it denotes not only "you" singular (the communing person), but also "you" plural (meaning "all"). In a fuller practice of the sacrament we might say, "This is the body of Christ given for you," looking the communicant in the eye, "and for you," raising the arms as if to embrace the entirety of the assembly gathered, the entirety of humanity, and the entirety of creation. Indeed the Sacrament of the Table is the Word and visible sign of God's active unmerited love for the person receiving it and *also* of God's active unmerited love for all. Now, as I share the bread and wine, I realize that Christ is coming to "you" for "you," and also that Christ is coming into "you" for the sake of the world; Christ is coming into us through the power of the Spirit, so that we may embody Christ as active love for the world. Now, as I hold each communicant in view and in prayer, I see her or him as part of a cloud of witnesses sent forth as Christ's body to bring healing and liberation. What, I wonder, would this church be like, if in receiving the bread and the wine, all the baptized saw and heard that it was given *for* them as persons and *to* them for the healing of the world!

"To Proclaim the Good News of God in Christ through Word and Deed"

This church is called to proclaim the gospel in and to *the world;* proclamation is intrinsically public. We proclaim both our need for God's grace and the gift of God's grace, the Word of God revealing divine judgment and mercy. The heart of this proclamation, as expressed in Lutheran traditions, is justification by grace alone through faith alone. God in Christ has saved us from death, sin, and the devil through no merit of our own. Salvation is only by God's grace through faith. That faith, likewise, is a gift from God.

It is given by God through the Spirit, in the living Christ proclaimed. "Faith . . . is a divine work in us which changes us and makes us altogether different . . . Faith is a living, daring confidence in God's grace, so sure and certain that the believer would stake his life on it a thousand times."[19]

Lutherans have reveled in rich and diverse theological inquiry into the full meaning and implications of justification. Being grounded firmly in the trust that we are made right with God by God, Lutherans around the world have sought to discern what this life-saving claim means for everyday life. Knowing that salvation is sure and is unearnable, Lutherans are freed from worry about salvation and freed to probe the infinitely rich consequences of God's unconditional and boundless love for this world, revealed most fully in Jesus Christ born, crucified, and risen: the living Christ with, in, and among us.

Vital in that inquiry and germane in this discussion of proclamation have been conversations regarding the public significance of justification. That theological inquiry, as most, has multiple and finely nuanced perspectives. For some, justification has little public import; the significance of justification is private. In the face of God's judgment on our sin as individuals, God makes individuals right with God in God's eyes. Justification does not change us in terms of societal relationships, and does not refer directly to structural sin or to the salvation of people and the rest of creation from it. From another perspective, redemption of individuals from their sin and redemption from social structural sin are intertwined, and justification pertains to both.

These two portrayals are done in broad strokes and do not do justice to the complexity and depth of the positions they illustrate. They are joined by other perspectives. Consistent throughout them is the conviction that sin as *se incurvatus in se* inevitably inhabits the realm of human relationships—hence the *simul justus et peccator* eschatology affirmed in Lutheran theology. The right relations on earth, given by God in Christ, are never *fully* realized until the end times. The reign of God is both already and not yet.

The question of justification's public significance has come to the fore with the rise of Lutheran theological voices in non-Western cultures and of Lutheran feminist voices in the North Atlantic world. In a recent

Lutheran World Federation volume, *Justification in the World's Context,*[20] Lutherans from different cultural, political, and ecclesial realities world-wide speak with each other and with the broader Lutheran communion regarding interpretations of our central proclamation. The result is a rich, theologically sophisticated, and provocative invitation to consider the social impacts of how Luther's and the confessors' central doctrine is understood. As public church in a global public, and as part of a larger body of Christ, the Lutheran church in North America will continue in that conversation with its sister and brother churches around the globe. As a church composed of people from extraordinarily varied contexts in North America, we also will invite theological reflection on that central proclamation from varied social locations within the ELCA. Indeed, true to our roots of theological inquiry grounded in the living Word, this church will ask and probe—through prayer, study, and action—what all is given in this gift of unconditional and unearnable love, and what it means for our witness as public church at the dawn of the 21st century.

"Proclamation . . . includes the *public* reading of Scripture"[21] (italics mine) as "the basis for the public proclamation of the Gospel."[22] This claim, made and heard in a pluralistic society, startles. By what creative paths will this church better equip its members for this dimension of our vocation? "Proclamation . . . includes . . . confession and absolution."[23] Confession, in the Lutheran church, is a public act in a dual sense. First, it is part of public worship. Second, confessing our sin includes confessing our failures to live the gospel in public. How might we draw more deeply on the power of confession and absolution in public life? Evidence is mounting that lament and confession are aspects of social healing, perhaps necessary aspects. Who is better suited to initiate and lead public confession and lament for the social sins of our day than a people who confess—on a regular basis—the pervasive presence of sin, forgiveness as gift from God, and God's reconciling and healing power? "Proclamation . . . includes . . . Christian witness, and service."[24] To this our attention moves shortly.

Proclamation of the Word is two-sided. It involves both telling the story and hearing it. We are called to hear and trust the good news again and again, as well as to tell it. Consider the "hearing," for it often is less attended in discussions of proclamation. Through whom are we summoned to hear the gospel? Who proclaims it? "The richest text studies of my life," attests one Lutheran pastor, "were my weekly Bible studies with a group of homeless women recovering from severe substance abuse. Having expected to witness to them, I heard the Word through them."[25] Knowing that all faith claims are interpreted through cultural lenses, and having learned in recent decades that our understanding of the gospel is enriched and deepened by interpretations formed through "other" lenses, this public church will open new ways to hear the gospel proclaimed from diverse social and geographic locations within the ELCA and in the broader Christian community.

An ancient tenet of Christian faith holds that prayer and liturgy not only are shaped by belief and faithful action, but also shape them. Doctrine and deeds are to be consistent with prayer and liturgical praise of God. *Lex orandi est lex credendi et agendi* ("The rule of prayer is the rule of belief and action"). Prayer and liturgy may reveal previously unrecognized dimensions of proclamation. In worship, Lutherans "sing with all the people of God and join in the hymn of all creation."[26] This provocative liturgical gift beckons us to join with ecumenical sisters and brothers in sharing the good news, both as hearers and as tellers, and it invites this church to ponder the boundaries of who or what proclaims the gospel. Will the church of our day explore more fully the biblical testimony that God calls upon the creatures and elements of earth to "testify," "witness," "minister" (Ps.104:4), convey God's message (Ps. 104:4), and praise God (Ps. 148)? Ponder two faith claims, held in light of each other. First, in Luther's words, "Christ . . . fills all things . . . Christ is around us and in us in all places . . . [H]e is present in all creatures, and I might find him in stone, in fire, in water . . . for he certainly is there . . ."[27] Second, the work of Christ—wherever Christ is—is to create, save, and sustain. Held in one breath, these two faith affirmations pose questions: Will this public church venture into the uncharted terrain of asking how human creatures may hear the Word of God spoken through other-kind? Might our proclamation reach human hearts yet closed to it, if we begin to listen for the voice of winds (Ps. 104:4) and waters (Ps. 148) singing "the hymn of all creation," and hence—in some way not yet grasped by us—proclaiming the good news of God in Christ?

"To Serve All People, Following the Example of Our Lord Jesus"; "To Strive for Justice and Peace in All the Earth"

In Lutheran traditions, the call to serve all people and to strive for justice and peace are understood as expressions of the call to "love neighbor as self."[28] This understanding, deeply rooted in Scripture, is elaborated in Lutheran theological terms by Luther, and eloquently so. Luther identifies "two principles of Christian doctrine."[29] The first principle is that Christ gave himself that we may be saved, and we are saved by no effort of our own. The second "is love . . . as he gives himself for us . . . so we too are to give ourselves with might and main for our neighbor."[30] Luther insists on the inseparability of the two: they are "inscribed together as on a tablet which is always before our eyes and which we use daily."[31] He preaches, "God makes love to our neighbor an obligation equal to love to himself."[32] Many in this church know this "second principle" as "faith active in love." "Faith is not the human notion and dream that some people call faith . . . O it is a living, busy, active, mighty thing this faith. It is impossible for it not to be doing good works incessantly."[33]

This insistence that active love for others is central to Christian faith—present in Luther's sermons, treatises, biblical exegesis, and catechetical writings—does not contradict his bottom line and consistent polemic against the scholastics and the church of Rome in his day: one is *not* justified by one's works of love or by any other form of "work."[34] Human creatures cannot contribute to their salvation. That is God's work in Christ. Rather, Luther's insistence that all human relations are to be normed by neighbor-love reflects his understanding of what happens through God's power when people are made righteous by God.

When made righteous, people are given "two kinds of righteousness." The "first" changes our relationship with God: we are totally forgiven and become righteous in God's sight. This is "alien righteousness,"[35] the righteousness of God in the righteousness of Christ. "[I]nstilled from without . . . [it is] given to men in baptism and whenever they are repentant."[36] After this first gift, God changes our relationships with other people through the "second kind of righteousness . . . our proper righteousness,"[37] which is the "product . . . fruit and consequence" of the first.[38] The second kind of righteousness is a "whole way of living" that includes living "justly with neighbor."[39] "Faith," Luther teaches, "is a divine work in us which changes us."[40]

The implications of "neighbor-love" for the life of the public church depend upon what is meant by the term.[41] Biblical "neighbor-love" bears at least the following marks. It implies active commitment to the well-being of who or what is loved. While love at its best includes delight, tenderness, life-giving passions, compassion, and deep pleasure, the fundamental attribute of love from a biblical perspective is steadfast, enduring commitment to seek the good of who or what is loved. Next, where systemic injustice causes suffering,[42] seeking the well-being or good of those who suffer entails challenging that injustice. The challenge includes seeing systemic evil for what it is and acknowledging it, resisting it, and pioneering[43] more just alternatives.[44] In short, the norm of neighbor-love *includes* the norm of justice.[45] Thirdly, the biblical command of neighbor-love is constructed brilliantly to presuppose the normativity of self-love: "you shall love your neighbor as yourself."[46] And finally, biblically-based neighbor-love implies a splendid mutuality. Not only are we called to serve the well-being of others, but also to receive that care from others. Neighbor-love is "more than the strong serving the weak which may lead to paternalistic assumptions and practices,"[47] and may imply that some are not able to serve. Jesus modeled the gift of *receiving* others' loving care, as well as giving it.

According to Luther, neighbor-love, as the norm for public life, has at least three dimensions:

- love manifest in service to neighbor, even if it may bring great danger to self and family;[48]
- love manifest in disclosing and theologically denouncing oppression or exploitation of those who are vulnerable, where it is perceived;[49] and
- love manifest in ways of living that counter prevailing cultural norms where those norms exploit the vulnerable or defy God in some other way.

Loving in these forms, "we become hands and feet of Christ, for the healing of the world."[50]

Luther's commitment to neighbor-love as service to those is need (the first of the dimensions of love listed above) was displayed in his response to the question of whether or not a Christian may flee from a town if it were infested with the deadly plague. Luther responded that a Christian could flee only if no one needed her or his assistance! (Of course, in the midst of the plague, there always would be someone who needed help, so a Christian could not flee.) He and Kathryn indeed nursed the ill in their home during the plague, putting at risk themselves and their children.

One aspect of public-life regarding which the three dimensions of neighbor-love are evident in Luther is economic life. According to Luther, economic activity is intrinsically an act in relationship to neighbor, and all relations with neighbor are normed by one thing: the Christian is to serve the neighbor's well-being in multiple ways, while also meeting the needs of self and household. About this Luther was vehement and specific, in theology and in practice. He helped to establish a local social welfare system that provided material goods and created jobs for the unemployed. He theologically denounced certain aspects of the emerging capitalist economy that exploited the poor of his day and admonished preachers to do the same.[51] Finally, Luther taught that widely accepted economic norms and practices that undermined the widespread good or the well-being of the poor ought to be eschewed in daily practice and replaced with alternatives. As alternatives, Luther established norms for everyday economic life that prioritized meeting human needs over maximizing profit as the central aim of economic life. For example, Christians, according to Luther's economic norms, must refuse to charge what the market will bear when selling products, if so doing jeopardizes others' well-being.[52] Christians may not buy essential commodities when the price is low and sell when it is high, for so doing endangers the poor.[53]

Historically, this church has been admirably apt in the first of these, and (as far as I am aware) has adopted it, without dissent, as normative for the church's life. Often, we have been more reticent in the latter two dimensions of neighbor-love. As a whole, we have been better prepared to "serve all people" than to "strive for justice and peace in all the earth." Yet, the ELCA commits itself also to the latter. The document, "Vision and Expectations: Ordained Ministers in the Evangelical Lutheran Church in

America,"[54] explains that, among many elements of "faithful witness," "this church expects its ordained ministers to be witnesses to and be instruments of God's peace and reconciliation for the world . . . The church is to witness to God's call for justice in every aspect of life, including testimony against injustice and oppression, whether personal or systemic. This church expects its ordained ministers to be committed to justice in the life of the church, in society, and in the world."[55] According to the ELCA constitution, the Division for Global Mission will "cooperate with the global community in promoting justice and the equitable sharing of resources."[56] The Division for Church in Society is charged with "seeking to promote justice, peace, and the care of the earth."[57]

This commitment to seek justice is not surprising, for Lutheranism bears a rich heritage and theological basis for justice-making. Luther and the confessors were suspicious of any authority or power thwarting Christians' right relationships *coram Deo* and *coram mundo* ("before God" and "before the world"). Today as then, such powers may be political, economic, military, or cultural structures. Where they require exploitative relationships, these structures preclude "right relationships." The summons to love neighbor, then, includes a summons to unmask and challenge those social structures. Where public structures or acts of oppression[58] are theologically justified, it is the unique justice-making responsibility of the church to disclose, repent of, and undo those theological rationales.

The call to strive for justice is clarion. What it means for the life of this church is not. In the ELCA, we speak of "justice" frequently and sincerely. It has become almost commonplace, bearing a sense of certainty and rightness. With the words however, the simplicity ends. "Justice" is a multilayered and complex term with multiple formal meanings and myriad connotations. It cries out for explication.

"Justice" has a millennia-long and highly contested history. Its connotations and denotations shift and evolve depending upon context. New meanings often are grounded in critique of established and assumed meanings. Fortunately, the mark of the baptized is not to *agree* on the meaning of "justice," but only that the people of God are called to "strive for" it "in all the earth." However, a serious commitment to heed this mark of the baptized inevitably leads to the question, What does the church mean when it claims "striving for justice in all the earth" as integral to its witness to the love of God? What does this claim mean for the life of the church in its various contexts? Sorting out the range of referents to arrive at a normative theological understanding of "justice" cannot be the intent here. Rather, I simply highlight a few dimensions of the term and its history that may assist this church as it continues in the difficult and faithful task of discerning what it means in any given circumstance to "strive for justice." Classical and modern Western notions of justice, more recent criticisms of them, theological and biblical notions of justice, and documents of the ELCA—in that order—inform this brief inquiry.

Justice is a central moral norm in Western thought and is theorized in philosophical ethics, political theory, Christian ethics, and other dimensions of Christian theology. In its most ancient sense justice referred to a power that maintained right relationship in the cosmos, including but not limited to human life. As ancient Greek society and philosophy developed, justice pertained more specifically to the human world. Conceived of as a virtue of society, it consisted of institutions ordered so as to promote the virtue of individuals, social harmony, and happiness. Aristotle distinguished three broad categories of justice:[59]

- Commutative justice focussing on transactions between individuals, both voluntary (for example, the exchange of goods and services) and involuntary (for example, theft);
- Distributive justice assuring the fair distribution of a society's or community's benefits (goods, rights) and burdens (responsibilities);
- Legal justice pertaining to the obligations of individuals to society.

Modern thought maintains these three categories and adds others, including "social justice" and "restitutional justice."[60] The former, notes Notre Dame theologian Richard McBrien, "is dedicated to the reordering of society, to the changing of institutions, systems, and patterns of behavior which deny people their basic human rights and which thereby destabilize society."[61] "Social justice seeks to provide for the full and fair participation of all persons and groups in the governance of political, economic, cultural, and social institutions, and aims at correcting any oppressive and alienating trends within the community. Where there is not social justice, there probably is not much distributive, commutative, or legal justice either . . ."[62] Restitutional justice seeks to make amends through retribution or reparation to victims of injustice.

Understandings of justice as a moral norm for public life[63] have been influenced notably by the mid-twentieth century public theologian, Reinhold Niebuhr, and his insistence on the immoral nature of human societies; sin inevitably is manifest in societies as the power of some groups, exercised in the service of self-interest, over others. Justice, presupposing that context, referred to balancing the competing claims and powers of those groups, and balancing between claims for liberty and claims for equality (a tension present in United States democracy since its inception).[64] Moral philosopher, John Rawls, in the early 1970s, theorized justice as the impartial assignment of rights, duties, and benefits on the basis of established societal agreements to members of a society who participate in it on a free and equal basis. Justice in this sense was understood as universally applicable. The stress was on fairness and impartiality, and not on a human right to certain goods and rights. Note, here too, an essential presupposition: this notion of justice assumes a society in which people indeed have the capacity to participate equally in shaping the terms of public life.

Modern notions of justice and the presuppositions undergirding them have come under strong critique in the last three decades. Those criticisms are inaugurating five shifts in understandings of justice, relevant to the church as agent of justice. One move identifies the error in assuming that all members of a society are equal in resources and the opportunity to participate in shaping the agreements governing public life. The second is closely related. It moves from justice applied impartially without consideration for power differentials and historical factors, to a sense that justice may have different demands depending on what side of power one is located. Third is a shift in distributive justice to include not only distribution of goods, responsibilities, and burdens, but also distribution of power.[65] Fourth is the sense that what constitutes justice is best known through the experience of injustice or through struggles to overcome it.[66] The final development pertains to the scope of justice; historically pertaining to human relations, justice increasingly is seen as relevant (although in yet undefined ways) to the entire web of life on earth.

Theological and ecclesiological developments are contributing to these monumental shifts. In turn, these shifts contribute to the ongoing development of justice as a norm in Christian life. Theologically informed claims about justice (a rather thin translation of the Hebrew *sedaqah* and *mispat)* draw on classical and modern theories of justice and critiques of them, but they draw also on biblical and theological sources. Theological interpretations and uses of "justice" are diverse and stand in varying degrees of tension with theories of justice in law and political philosophy. Christian discourse tends to focus on "social justice" and "structural justice" (aims at structural inequalities in a society) as a dimension of it.

One seed of this focus is Pope Leo XIII's landmark encyclical, "The Condition of Labor" *(Rerum Novarum)* 1891. With this letter and its significant follow-up of 40 years later,[67] "social justice"—as concern for the common good and for the well-being of economically poor people—entered the discourse. Vatican II (1962-1965) and the subsequent Conference of Latin American Bishops (1968 and 1979) paved the way for a theological claim that God's justice indeed is *not* impartial. It leans toward the needs and plight of the poor, and calls followers of Jesus to identify with those who are marginalized, dehumanized, or otherwise oppressed. This assertion—termed "preferential option for the poor"—is grounded in Jesus' identification with the marginalized, and in the Hebrew Bible.[68] In Scripture, the Hebrew words *sedaqah* (justice, righteousness) and *mispat* (justice, right), when combined, best approximate the moral implications of justice. Both are rich and textured terms; neither is adequately translated by any single English word. *Sedaqah* refers to right relationships between God and God's people, between persons, and between groups ("groups" here includes societies, as well as smaller collections of people). Right relations are those that allow the needs of all to be met in a way in which the relationship can flourish and community can be preserved. The character of *sedaqah* "is known in God's actions to establish Israel in deliverance and preserve community in covenant."[69] *Mispat* has judicial implications and also "has a broader meaning dealing with the rights due to every individual in the community, and the upholding of those rights."[70]

While interpretations of justice as a Christian moral norm vary, many who use it would agree that "justice" as a norm grounded in Scripture

- is a chief attribute of God's activity in the world;[71]
- is based on and corresponds to the justice of God which is seen as liberating the oppressed, identifying with the vulnerable and upholding their rights, judgment, and mercy;
- is integral to love of neighbor, but not synonymous with it;
- is a foundation of the "already but not yet reign" of God;
- implies compassion and redistribution, with special attention to the needs of the marginalized;
- aims at freeing the oppressed, sharing food with the hungry, housing the homeless, and more;
- aims also at dismantling the sources of oppression and the political, cultural, and economic arrangements that contribute to hunger, poverty, and homelessness;
- is understood to be both demand of God and gift from God;
- was not, at least in the prophets, understood as a utopian impossibility, but as realizable.[72]

Justice, then, in a biblical sense is not so much a goal as a grounding orientation that affects how a church relates to its own structures and practices, its context, the world, and its God-given calling. "This basic orientation is reflected in a continual probing that asks of any situation, what's wrong with this picture? What is unjust or unfair in how relationships are ordered in it? What stirs up indignation, anger, or even rage? What cries out for change?"[73] The orientation is one that draws no contrast between justice-making and personal piety, but holds both as reflections of "right relationship" with the God revealed in the stories of the ancient Hebrews with God, the workings of the Holy Spirit, and in Jesus Christ.

Holding in mind these glimpses into classical, modern, critical, and theological efforts to grasp the implications of "justice" for the church's life on earth, we turn finally to the ELCA's recent writings. What guidance do they offer for the doing of justice by assemblies of baptized believers? This church understands that an ingredient of "faithful witness"[74] is to "witness to God's call for justice in every aspect of life, including testimony against injustice and oppression, whether personal or systemic . . . justice in the life of the church, in society, and in the world."[75] This statement, together with others in the constitution, is replete with clues. The justice that we are to seek is justice as God calls for it. Our charge is to "witness to," "be committed to," "promote," "strive for," "and call for" justice.[76] So doing includes—but is not limited to—speaking "publicly to the world in solidarity with the poor and oppressed," [77] and offering "testimony against injustice and oppression, whether personal or systemic . . ." We are to seek justice not only in the broader "society" and "world," but also "in the life of the church." We of North America are to do so in cooperation with the global community. The particulars of those broad guidelines offered by the church will "grow out of the concrete, lived experiences of injustice in particular contexts, which have their own histories and call for their own forms of address."[78]

The call to "strive for justice and peace" is fraught with ambiguity. The task of faith-based moral discernment is called to the fore. In a world in which evil masquerades as good, in which all alternatives to an unjust situation may themselves be tainted with injustice, in which what brings well-being to some vulnerable people may bring damage to others, and in which the pernicious presence of sin invades human good—in such a world, the call to dismantle injustice *as an act of Christ-bearing love* is a summons to the difficult and daring art of faith-based moral discernment. That task is explored in chapter 5.

Today the Lutheran communion worldwide calls for weaving together service and justice-making. Lutheran diaconal ministers from around the world, gathered for a "Global Consultation on *Diakonia*," issued a compelling "Epistle," declaring,

> We acknowledge with gratitude the many kinds of diaconal work that the Church has carried out through the centuries, and which necessarily continues in our own day. This work is now challenged to move toward more prophetic forms of diakonia. Inspired by Jesus and the prophets who confronted those in power and called for changes in unjust structures and

practices, we pray that God may empower us to help transform all that leads to human greed, violence, injustice, and exclusion . . . While diakonia begins as unconditional service to the neighbor in need, it leads inevitably to social change that restores, reforms, and transforms.[79]

Indeed the ELCA's multiple forms of embodied neighbor-love (service, advocacy, community-based organizing, public protest, etc.) already are interdependent. They need each other as different complementary fingers on the hand of neighbor-love.

One soon finds that "to serve . . . following the example of our Lord Jesus" and "to strive for justice and peace" is to encounter heartrending suffering. We would much rather flee in the other direction. Yet the cross insists that we are people of a humiliated and broken God, a God revealed most fully and known most intimately and truly where life is tortured and broken.[80] It is this Christ with whom, in baptism, we die and rise, and this Christ who comes to dwell in and among God's people. The significance of the incarnation and the cross, in light of the call to serve and work toward justice and peace, stuns. If the church is to be what it is, and is to know this God, we will not run from suffering at the cost of failing to serve neighbors in need or failing to seek justice and peace in all the earth.[81] Furthermore, the power to serve others in the midst of their suffering abides in those who love with the indwelling love of Christ, a love undeterred by suffering. Presently we will consider, in more depth, these and related implications of the cross.[82]

"You have made public profession of your faith. Do you intend to continue in the covenant God made with you in Holy Baptism . . . to serve all people, following the example of our Lord Jesus" and "to strive for justice and peace in all the earth?" The possible dangers and difficulties inherent in these dimensions of our life with God propel questions of moral-spiritual formation to the front-burner. What patterns of worship, Bible study, daily life tasks, work, and recreation will "form" this people of God for those dimensions of our life in God? How do we remain "moist" so that Word and wisdom may continue to work on us and in us, shaping us into people who heed God's call to "do justice, and to love kindness, and walk humbly with your God" (Micah 6:8)?

The call to service, justice-making, and peace-making is a gift from God to the church. Our faith forbears have struggled for millennia to understand, receive, and bear fruit with it. This church has made a commitment to follow in that stream. The meaning and demands of God's justice are for the church to probe and discern in good faith.

"To Live among God's Faithful People"

Lutheran traditions assume that it is possible to be God's faithful people only as an assembly of believers. The baptized have no option; in Baptism we are woven into the church, so "that we may" live our calling. In multiple ways, our lives depend upon living among God's faithful people: Jesus Christ comes to us through one another. God's Supper is "shared." Baptism is given by God through people in the presence of yet others. To be heard, the Word must be proclaimed. Proclamation is from one to another. Indeed, we receive the gospel and continue to receive it by "living among God's faithful people." The vows we make—in marriage, in Baptism, in ordination—are not made privately; they are witnessed by God's faithful people. Only by "living among" them can we hold one another accountable to those vows and support one another in faithfulness to them. How fascinating that the "you" addressed in the New Testament is almost exclusively a plural "you." Indeed, to be alive, as we are reborn in Baptism, is a communal reality. Here we venture further into the mystery of the "assembly" we call church. We are woven together as church by profound mutual need. In today's modern and postmodern public life, where privatized spirituality and religion abound, the church says not only "I," but also "we." Our power to be who we are and to live out our vocation, our power to be public church in public life, is given and nourished by God through the faith community. A public church will nourish its congregations as the most intimate expression of this assembly.

To live among God's faithful people, to be church, is to be and live *as body of Christ*. By the power of the Holy Spirit, in Baptism ". . . we are made members of the body of Christ, the Church."[83] As expressed by Dietrich Bonhoeffer, the church is "Christ existing as community." "'[T]o be in Christ' is the same as 'to be in the community' . . . The community is the body of Christ, but only under the gathering and uniting influence of the

Holy Spirit."[84] Throughout his adulthood, Bonhoeffer grappled with the implications of this identity for the church's role in public life. They are perhaps infinite, beyond full human knowing, and unfold distinctly in differing contexts. For now, let us say this: In probing our role in public life, we probe what it means to *be Christ's body—a people of the incarnation*—in public. This church will equip its people for life-long discernment regarding the shape of life as Christ's body. "What," we must query, "are the ingredients of that discernment process?" To this question we will return in this inquiry's final chapter.

For the ELCA, "to live among God's faithful people" is to be part of a worldwide Lutheran "communion." The Lutheran World Federation—A Communion of Churches,[85] at its 1990 Assembly in Curitiba, recognized itself as a "communion" of churches,[86] holding in common "baptism, as our primary ordination, a Gospel centered in unmerited grace, and a common global mission of justification and justice . . ."[87] Since then the LWF has been leading the Lutheran communion worldwide in exploring the implications of this *communio* identity for the life of a public church in this world of complex global interconnectedness. Congregations, teaching theologians, pastors, biblical scholars, youth, and other Lutherans the world over are engaging the inquiry. As a "communion," our movement has been toward deeper relationships of accountability, interdependence, responsibility, and mutuality in work to further God's mission. One implication is an emerging awareness that the various Lutheran churches need one another's support in discerning *how* God is calling each member church to use its particular gifts for the "healing of the world"[88] and other dimensions of proclaiming the gospel. A solid principle of Christian discernment is that voices of people on the margins of power and privilege be heard. Dietrich Bonhoeffer put it well: "There remains an experience of incomparable value . . . to see . . . from below, from the perspectives of the outcast, the suspects, the maltreated, the powerless, the oppressed, the reviled—in short, from the perspectives of those who suffer."[89] For, the ELCA, a member of the Lutheran communion situated in, arguably, the world's most powerful nation, this principle opens doors. In discerning faithful response to public issues with global significance, for example, the summons is to seek the input and perspectives of sister churches in less powerful nations and in locations where people are suffering in relationship to the issue under consideration, and to listen carefully to their concerns and requests.

What does this mean for the ELCA? The question is at once daunting and exhilarating. Lutherans worldwide include indigenous people and those whose ancestors colonized them, extraordinarily wealthy people and highly impoverished people, people in seats of power and people actively challenging those power structures. Luther claims that in the Sacrament of the Table all self-seeking love is rooted out and gives place to that which seeks the common good of all. We come to the table to take upon ourselves each other's burdens, and are, in fact, "changed into" one another. How do we even begin to think about being a church that "seeks the common good of all," truly "shares burdens," and is "changed into" the other, when some of our brothers and sisters are among the Dalit and tribal people of India? They are being displaced from the homelands that have sustained them for generations by the Bauxite mines that produce metals upon which our daily routines depend? What will we hear if, in discerning the shape of our public mission, we consult the members of our body in Brazil, in Liberia, in Palestine? Have we the courage to open our eyes and ears? What will we do with what we learn? How are we to see and hear from perspectives that we may not yet know exist? How will we learn to do so?

A crucial step is the effort to "see the eyes through which we see." People of relatively dominant cultures tend to perceive reality through the lens of their own cultural position. That lens is pulled almost irresistibly toward "universalizing" and "normalizing" its own perspectives, failing to recognize it as just one amongst multiple perspectives. To illustrate: in worship, the ELCA (as most Christian churches), celebrates the unity of the church, singing of it and praying for it. Yet, hear the words of Tore Johnson, a Sami Lutheran from the Church of Norway. (The Sami are the indigenous people in northern Norway, Sweden, Finland, and the Kola peninsula in Russia. Commonly their territory has been referred to as Lapland.)

> I want to share with you some of the Sami experience in Norway . . . Our experience as a minority is that the majority often lack fundamental cultural awareness. They simply consider their ways universal. Therefore we have often experienced how *dangerous it can be to welcome a well-intentioned*

invitation by the majority to "celebrate" our unity [italics mine]. We have experienced so many times that this meant to enter the fellowship on the premises of the majority. We had to leave ourselves behind. Now we are more recognized in the church. Important structural changes have been made. But we realize that it is still a long way to walk on the path of healing. It is hard especially because it demands a new mindset of the majority culture in the church . . . Are we willing to address the questions of cultural and theological hegemony in our Lutheran community.[90]

Living among God's faithful people in a world of stunning interconnection bids us find and face such questions and challenges, seeking faithful response. They are difficult, easily avoided. In the face of the inevitable fears or confusion, may this church be encouraged by recalling *why* we are a worldwide communion: to further God's mission in the world through our work together and through mutual edification and support. May we remember that God not only creates and calls this church to serve God's mission, God provides all that we need to do so, including the courage and capacity to open eyes and ears, and to enter new and uncharted terrain. Finally, may we grow in "bold undaunted courage" (the words are Luther's) trusting that God is within and among this communion, and that God's grace surpasses every force in heaven or on earth.

What might we expect as we grow more interdependent and mutually accountable within a worldwide Lutheran communion that is sent to proclaim justification and justice in a world in which death and oppression are the daily fare of many? Few things are surer than that a God made human in a peasant infant born amidst cow dung, tortured to death, spread "like a dew over all the earth," and "filling all things . . . even the tiniest leaf" will continue to astound the faithful with the unexpected! One ought not predict. Yet my sense is this: as the ELCA lives out ever more fully its relationships within this global communion, we might expect

- to encounter the cross of Jesus Christ and the resurrection in unforeseen forms;
- to meet the living God in places of profound joy, suffering, brokenness, healing, and liberation;

- our worship life to become more unsettling and life-giving;
- our theological assumptions to be jostled, honed, passed through refining fires; (The last three decades have seen a major shift in the way theology is done. A focus on normative foundational doctrinal stances has given way to a focus on the contextual nature of theology, especially as that context relates to the church in the world.[91] The nature of sin and salvation, the life of Jesus, and nature of the church, for example, may be understood differently from the perspective of a Lutheran church situated in San Salvador than for a largely well-off church in the United States. Key to negotiating this terrain will be the commitment to work constructively with "the tension between the gospel that holds us together and the diversity by which we express it."[92])
- our own doubts, discouragement, and despair to flair;
- our trust in God to be deepened;
- conflict and vexing cross-cultural miscommunication;
- our assumptions about the global economy and our practices of buying, selling, and investing to be disrupted;
- new depths and breadth in our understanding of service, justice, peace, Word, Supper, proclamation . . . marks of the baptized;
- distinctions between giver and recipient to be blurred and transgressed;
- our engagement in United States foreign policy to be requested by our sisters and brothers of the Two-thirds World;
- the growth of life-giving relationships through which we receive and give the living Christ;
- danger, and courage we did not know we had;
- to be cared for and prayed for abundantly.

The mark of the baptized is not to live only among God's faithful *Lutheran* people, but also to live in mutually edifying relationship with other assemblies in the body of Christ. What a profound ecumenical commitment we make in the covenant "to live among God's faithful people." This church will rejoice in the particular gifts of understanding and ministry that God has given to other parts of Christ's body on earth, and eagerly will share with them the gifts of the Lutheran tradition. We will "join with other Christians in prayer and action to express and preserve the unity which the Spirit gives" for the sake of God's mission.[93] These ecumenical commitments are grounded not only in recognition of our shared faith, but also in our growing recognition that, in many instances, our very differences are gifts. They enable each denominational member of the body to perceive more self-critically its own weaknesses and to value its particular contributions to the whole. In a word, exploring our differences, be they complementary or cautionary, may be edifying, enabling each part of the body to become more whole and more able to participate in God's work.

Compelling too, but historically less familiar, is the call to relationship with faith traditions other than Christian. Secure that God, and not human beings, knows where the Spirit blows, and aware of the danger lurking in religious self-righteousness, Lutherans do not claim to know the boundaries of "God's faithful people." Knowing that God's grace in Jesus Christ exceeds human comprehension, and acknowledging that as "stewards of God's mysteries" (1 Cor. 4:1) we neither glimpse them fully nor control them, a church called to "live among God's faithful people" will deepen and extend interfaith relationships for the sake of the world.

According to the covenant God makes with us in baptism, we are to "live among God's faithful people." As any committed member of a congregation can attest, the challenges of life together, even in a familiar Lutheran parish, drive one to prayer. Needless to say, daring the vicissitudes of life in global, ecumenical, and interfaith families renders prayer essential sustenance! We will be ever more a praying people. We will pray, giving thanks for the Sprit through whom God's communion overcomes all barriers that divide. We will pray—for self and in intercession—for the wisdom, patience, courage, and good humor required by life together.

About the power of prayer for enabling Christian vocation and Christian community, Luther is vehement. "Note how Paul devotes himself to the welfare of the Christian community," Luther implores, ". . . but we do not rightly heed his example . . . we do not avail ourselves to the Gospel's power in the struggles of life. Unquestionably the trouble is we do not earnestly pray."[94] "Paul desires Christ to be efficacious in the hearts of his followers . . . But the heart which has not yet arrived at this point is here advised what course to take, namely, to pray to God for such faith and strength, and to avail himself to the prayers of others to the same end."[95]

"[I]t is necessary for us continually to pray God to replace our weakness with courage, and to put into our hearts his Spirit to fill us with grace and strength and rule and work in us absolutely."[96] In all, we give thanks that our failures and shortcomings are forgiven in whole and that salvation is not the fruit of our efforts in the world, but rather those efforts are the fruit of salvation.

This journey through the marks of the baptized has illumined key dimensions of who we are as public church, our vocation, and how these shape the church's role in public life today. Questions for further inquiry have been raised. Two overarching questions warrant special attention. What obstacles impede the church from living out its public vocation? Wherein lies the moral-spiritual power for so living? We consider both illustratively in the following two chapters. Both are rooted staunchly in one central Lutheran faith conviction: as the church is gathered and sent, we are and always will be beloved and forgiven creatures of God. We can neither earn that grace nor escape it. Only as recipients of God's love are we called to embody it in this beautiful and broken world. Only as beloved, ever beloved, are we called to serve the well-being of self, others, and all of creation. The church is created and called first to receive the life-giving, life-saving, and life-sustaining love of God, and then to proclaim, witness to, and embody it in public life. No force in heaven or earth can separate this world from God's love revealed and given in Jesus Christ.

Questions for Reflection

1. What do you make of Luther's claim that "The Word of God wherever it comes, comes to change and renew the world"?

2. How are the Word that we hear and the Meal that we share connected with our public witness to the love of God in Christ Jesus?

3. The author states that "Word and Eucharist are ancient practices through which the living Christ comes to, into, and among the community of believers and there calls forth power for faith active in love, even if that love calls the faithful to swim upstream against torrential

and dangerous social forces." Re-read Luther's statements about the Eucharist on page 17. Recall a time when you have experienced Word or sacrament in these terms. Imagine that your congregation is pondering these words of Luther. What might be the impact on the worship life of your congregation? What would be the impact on other aspects of its life?

4. What impact is the proclamation of the good news of God's reign meant to have on the way that followers of Jesus Christ live in the world?

5. How can we "serve all people following the example of our Lord Jesus Christ," without putting ourselves in the role of patronizing or even dominating "the other"? Without "burning out"? Given the magnitude of human need, how do you discern whom to serve and when?

6. In what ways have you or your church community sought "peace and justice in all the earth"? In what ways have other Lutherans done so? What has held you back from doing so?

7. Discuss what it means to "live among God's faithful people" in your congregation, in your ecumenical community, in your city, in the worldwide Lutheran communion of churches, among people of other religions, and within the world. With whom among God's faithful people do you find it most challenging to relate?

3

Obstacles to Being Public Church in Public Life

As this church steps forth boldly as public church,[1] formidable obstacles stand in the way. Acknowledging and identifying them, in faith, is key to overcoming them. That vast undertaking exceeds the scope of this book. Here, we simply illustrate with a focus on impediments pertaining to two strands of the baptismal covenant: the commitments "to serve all people, following the example of our Lord Jesus," and "to strive for justice and peace in all the earth."

That we are called to "faith active in love" is standard fare for this church. The ELCA and its predecessor bodies have affirmed without dissension that (1) Christian life unfolds under the norm of neighbor-love; (2) neighbor-love includes attending to material well-being as well as spiritual; (3) neighbors extend beyond the Christian community to all of humankind;[2] and (4) love has a special task of seeking to ameliorate suffering. More importantly, this church has, in profound and significant ways, embodied those claims through service ministries in multiple and magnificent forms. Those ministries have been integral in the life of this church in all three of its primary expressions (congregations, synods, church-wide).

What then could explain the contradictory reality of Lutheran assemblies situated amongst "neighbors" suffering from varied forms of structural oppression, and yet not "loving" those neighbors by seeking to challenge the social structures, such as white racism, "unjust" warfare, or economic exploitation, that are degrading or tormenting them? How is it that a tradition so theologically rich in the call "to love neighbor as self," and so practically rich in embodying that love corporately through service ministries, rarely has forged ways of challenging social structural sources of unnecessary human suffering and offering alternatives? How is it that efforts to "strive for peace and justice" through public policy advocacy, resisting systemic injustice, and advocating systemic change have been greeted, at times, with suspicion?

We are theological heirs of a public and political theologian and pastor who wrote over one thousand letters to civil authorities, including letters regarding their public policies; fervently admonished preachers to *preach* against economic injustice and against economic practices and public policies that thwarted the well-being of the poor;[3] called for modes of trade and commerce that defied the emerging capitalism where it oppressed the poor; and insisted that if civil authorities call Christians to actions that disobey God, then Christians must resist. Grappling with the public realities and struggles of his day in light of the gospel, Luther spoke publicly regarding political, military, economic, and theological issues, and took stands on which he staked his life.

On what grounds could Lutheran communities in this heritage *not* expect their bishops, ordained pastors, and other members to be a public voice in public policy? Why has Lutheran tradition in the United States leaned toward marginalizing the moral life as it pertains to bodies politic and to the political body, where Luther held the public moral life at the center of Christian life? What explains the tendency toward moral passivity characteristic of many Lutheran churches in the face of structural sin?

Moral Anthropological Obstacles: "Selves Curved In on Self"

This predicament has one foot in our paradoxical existence as simultaneously sinner and justified.[4] The previous chapter considered Luther's conviction that in giving the "second kind of righteousness" and in giving Word and Eucharist,[5] God changes us toward being people who love neighbor as self. This sense of profound capacity for neighbor-love flowing from justification and from Word and Sacrament is met with Luther's equally strong insistence on the pervasive presence of sin, the humanly insurmountable reality of *se incurvatus in se* ("self curved in on self").

According to Luther, it is *not possible* for us to do the moral good as fully as we try to do it.

Selves turned in on self is a strikingly descriptive and deeply truthful account of our human reality. While the ELCA is a church of both wealthy and impoverished people, as a body we are positioned in relative economic privilege in two senses. First, many among us are not impoverished. Second, as a body we are part of—not autonomous from—the mainstream culture of the United States, a society with enormous material wealth in a world where many die of poverty. Luther's paradoxical moral anthropology speaks directly to the heart of life for people positioned in relative privilege in the global community today. Collectively, we may long to live according to justice-making, self-honoring love for earth and neighbor. We may yearn to live without exploiting neighbor or earth. But look at us. We are a species destroying the very life-support systems (for example, air, water, soil, and forests) upon which all life depends. Our society is so addicted to consumption-oriented ways that we close our hearts and minds to the death and destruction required to sustain them. Have we heard the chorus of voices from around the globe crying out that, in the words of Mozambique's Methodist Bishop Bernardino Mandlate, our consumer privilege is "bought with the blood of African children"[6] and of other impoverished people the world over? "Our children," declared a Mexican mother and strawberry picker, "die of hunger because our land, which ought to grow food for them, produces strawberries for your tables."[7]

Luther's insistence that *we are selves curved in on self*, unable to be otherwise, is a crucial dialectical partner to his opposing anthropological claim: having been filled with the Holy Spirit and fed in the eucharist, *we are no longer selves curved in on self; we are people who, with Christ's love, serve the widespread good.* Recall Luther's declaration: ". . . by means of this sacrament [Eucharist], all self-seeking love is rooted out and gives place to that which seeks the common good of all"[8] (this claim is grounded firmly in Luther's understanding of Christ "abiding in" believers, to be discussed in chapter 4). This *simul justus et peccator* moral anthropology insists that justification as morally empowering for public life is *not* justification as moral perfection, now or ever in earthly life. Our vocation to embody Christ's life-saving love in public must *not* be accompanied by any illusions of human perfectibility. The church remains simultaneously sin-ners and righteous. We are "rusty tools"[9] "on which God yet works daily and makes arrangements."[10]

This church, as it probes the mystery of being the body of Christ in public life, might be wise to pursue further the interplay of these two par-adoxical moral anthropological claims in our heritage. We are selves ded-icated   primarily   to   self-glorifying   and   self-serving   lives;   yet, simultaneously, through Christ we are freed from that bondage and freed for serving the good of all. How is it that North Atlantic Lutheranism has tended to let the former eclipse the latter, to let our identity as sinners overshadow our identity as people changed by God toward lives of service and justice-making? How might honoring both identities more fully impact the church's moral-spiritual power for justice-seeking neighbor-love as public witness?

Social and Theological Obstacles

The penchant toward moral passivity in the public sphere has countless social and theological roots. Uncovering them is a theological task facing the ELCA in the years to come. Here, we briefly note three influential fac-tors, and then consider three others in more depth.

First, some forms of faith active in love in public life are risky to our perceived unity. To illustrate, ordained pastors who long to heed the church's expectation that they testify "against injustice and oppression,"[11] may fear alienating congregational members by that testimony. The concern is well founded, for many of our congregations are not yet equipped for faith-based modes of moral discernment and conflict management that such testimony requires. Second, some Lutherans perceive certain theological dangers to be grave. These include the risks of instrumentalizing the church and of appearing to subordinate grace to works. A third factor is the tendency to disassociate the biblical norm of neighbor-love from the biblical norm of justice, a move that is suspect from a Lutheran theological perspective.

Fourth, is it possible that today despair and hopelessness lure us away from the call to "serve all people . . . and seek justice and peace in all the earth"? We live in dangerous times. I allude not to the danger of war or terrorism. I mean the danger of what happens to compassionate and aware people called to love neighbor through serving and seeking justice and peace, when we experience powerlessness in the face of systemic sin. It is the danger of giving up in subtle resignation or hopelessness. It is the terrible temptation to forget who we are and why we are assembled and sent by God. Despair and hopelessness may be the most cunning seductions we face, drawing us away from our vocation of service and justice-making. They may be most dangerous social illnesses of our day.[12] Hopelessness and despair are potent and multidimensional forces,[13] subtly luring Christians and others to believe that we cannot really help to heal public brokenness. Indeed, for compassionate Christians who take seriously the call to "faith active in love" in a global public, opening their hearts and minds to the "data of despair"[14]—the realities of suffering in this beautiful and broken world—may be to drown in it. Closed hearts and minds, moral oblivion, is far more bearable. That failing, numbness sets in. Where numbness thaws, despair makes sense. Holy outrage and lament are dead before born, and we hide our despair regarding systemic sin under the comforting cloak of virtue in private life or of privatized spirituality. Our witness in public is truncated. In this context Lutheran theology brings hope, as discussed in the following two chapters.

Yet another significant factor may be North Atlantic Lutheranism's theological reticence to consider seriously the social justice effects of justification, as well as its impact on moral agency. We tend to claim the comfort of justification by faith alone, while eschewing its ethical implications. We may cling fervently with good reason to justification, while not acknowledging its consequences for how all aspects of life are lived. Lutheranism in the North Atlantic world has leaned toward disconnecting salvation from its impact on public life.

> Moral agency, for the purposes of this book, is understood in moral philosophical terms as the power to serve the widespread good—prioritizing the needs of the most vulnerable—and in theological terms as the power to embody a fundamental moral norm of Christian life. That norm is active love for creation, where creation includes self, others,

and the rest of nature, and where love implies serving the well-being of the beloved, which may call for challenging systemic injustice. Moral agency then refers to the power to orient life around the well-being of communities and the planetary web of life, emphasizing the concerns of the vulnerable. Moral agency is the power to live toward the flourishing of the *oikos* (the entirety of God's created household). To so so is to live in ways that promote social and ecological well-being, prioritizing the concerns of the most vulnerable and Earth's regenerative health. It is to move toward lifestyles, relationships, policies, and structures that build communities characterized by compassion, social justice, and ecological sustainability. Moral agency, then, is the power to live—in life's multiple dimensions—in ways that serve not only the needs of self and family, but also the ongoing well-being of the larger Earth community, and in ways that do not contribute to unnecessary suffering and do not threaten Earth's capacity to sustain life for generations to come. In this book, moral agency, moral-spiritual agency, and moral-spiritual power are used interchangeably, where agency is understood to be given by God through Christ and Holy Spirit.[15]

The theological underpinnings of this proclivity are many and complex. This church has sought to unfold them. In continuing that effort, probing the following tendencies might be fruitful. One is the pull toward reducing justification to its forensic dimension,[16] neighbor-love to the believer's grateful response to justification, and law to the antithesis of gospel. Related is a penchant toward

- disassociating the "two kinds of righteousness," and obscuring the second;
- disconnecting the "two principles of Christian doctrine" (which, Luther insisted, are "inscribed *together* as on a tablet"[17] [italics mine]), and minimizing the second;

- detaching Jesus Christ as savior from Jesus Christ as transformer of the moral life, and denying the latter; and
- bifurcating the person as justified individual from the person as historical social being.

Together, these theological leanings craft a formula for moral quietude in the face of social structural sin.

A sixth and final factor undergirding reticence to challenge injustice in public life may be a Lutheran theological fault line pointed out by Dietrich Bonhoeffer in his *Letters and Papers from Prison,* and less explicitly in his *Ethics.* Rightly claiming Luther's *answer* (justification by grace alone through faith alone) as true for all time, we have centralized and sacralized Luther's *question,* the burning question in the public ethos of *his* day, as though that question were the burning question of *our* day also! Luther and the shapers of the Augsburg Confession were thoroughly contextual theologians. Luther's theo-ethical and political positions were rooted in his anguished struggle with central, burning public issues of his context. One of those issues was the perceived threat of eternal damnation. Luther spoke the gospel, the living Christ, in direct response to a paramount form of brokenness, sin, and oppression of his time: people believed that they were condemned if they did not earn God's favor. Luther wrestled with Scripture in relationship to this particular torment, which was deeply embedded in the public consciousness of his time and place.

Contemporary Lutherans and the broader public in the United States are not likely to be *as* tormented by this question as was the public of Luther's day. Many of us do not spend our waking hours sweating over the threat of eternal damnation. Generally speaking, we are not terrified—as was Luther—at a picture of Christ with the sword of judgment in his mouth. While Luther's people were distracted from God's promises by the fear of eternal damnation, contemporary North Americans are likely also to be distracted by other fears, forces, and anxieties. This church must continue to claim, proclaim, and probe the unfolding meaning, in *our* context, of Luther's breakthrough that justification is by grace alone through faith alone. We are challenged to do this without sacralizing the central theological question that he asked in his time, if so doing distracts us from asking questions that open hearts to the gospel and lead to social healing in our time. Faithfulness to God's mission is thwarted if we live in theological responses to the burning questions of a bygone context, to the exclusion of the compelling questions in our own. The danger is of limiting the gospel. If sin and human brokenness from God's gracious love assume different faces in different epochs and cultures, and if we are to proclaim the gospel in ours, then we must discern those faces in our contexts.

May this illustrative inquiry into obstacles that tempt this church away from our commitments to "serve all people" and "to and strive for justice and peace in all the earth" illumine the broader task of uncovering and facing impediments to living out all dimensions of the baptismal vocation. The task is a crucial one before the ELCA as public church. As James Baldwin notes, "Not everything that is faced can be changed, but nothing can be changed until it is faced."[18]

Questions for Reflection

1. Is it surprising to you to think of Martin Luther as a "public and political theologian and pastor who wrote over 1,000 letters to civil officials" and "admonished pastors to preach against economic injustice"? If so, how does this information affect you?

2. This chapter's opening paragraphs suggest that seeking peace and justice in all the earth includes recognizing unjust social systems—such as white racism, economic exploitation, or unjust war—that cause unnecessary suffering and challenging them? In what ways can you imagine doing this, as an outgrowth of your witness to the love of Jesus Christ?

3. What theological justification do we use to prevent ourselves from "seeking justice and peace in all the earth"?

4. What emotional conditions do we harbor that prevent us from "seeking justice and peace in all the earth"?

5. What social pressures do we encounter that prevent us from "seeking justice and peace in all the earth"?

6. What political realities do we face that prevent us from "seeking justice and peace in all the earth"?

4

Power for Being Public
Church in Public Life

Gazing long at the terrain of obstacles is dangerous unless done from the firm ground of central faith claims. The first claim is confidence that the one who gathers and sends this church in the world forgives us for all our failures and shortcomings in our stumbling attempts to be public church. Having faith, we have "a living daring confidence in God's grace."[1] Second, Lutheran theology maintains that the world is not ours; it is God's. Nor is the mission to which we are called ours; it too is God's. The assembly of believers is gathered and sent to give thanks for, witness to, and participate in *God's* mission in *God's* world.

Third, while Lutheran theological tradition insists on the ubiquitous presence of sin in human life, that insistence is held in dialectical tension with another truth: while in bondage to sin, we are at the same time freed from sin and are freed to participate in God's work in and for the world. The power that frees and sends the church is God's power. It is greater than the power of sin and of any obstacle faced by the church. In times of public despair regarding public life, it may be of utmost import for this church to name and claim the power *given by God in Christ and Spirit*. Our hope for the world is grounded there. The ELCA, as a public church seeking to discern God at work in this world after the ravages of the 20th century, is beckoned to traverse that theological landscape. Here we note a few promising paths.

Christ Abides in the Church; the Church Is Filled with Christ

"In Hebrew the word *abide* denotes 'to remain' or 'to dwell' in . . . Now this is a precious dwelling place and something to glory in, that through faith in Christ and through our eating, we . . . have Christ abiding in us with His might, power, strength, righteousness, and wisdom."[2] So wrote Luther. Scripture refers to the church as the body of Christ,[3] as does the Apology of the Augsburg Confession.[4] Indeed, this church confesses "to be somehow the body of the One born in a manger."[5]

Luther's conviction that Christ "abiding in" the communing community *is* the power for its life in public has gone underrecognized and undervalued. Explicitly expressed in Luther's sermons, theological treatises, and biblical exegesis, this faith claim is intriguing and fruitful for the task of exploring the power given to the church for the sake of God's mission in the world, the power enabling our public vocation.[6] Luther's writings ground this brief inquiry into the ancient faith claim that Christ "abiding in" the community of believers names not only who we are as church, but also our power to be who we are.

Hear Luther teaching and preaching Christ dwelling in the faithful, changing them into "servant of all," and rendering union and communion among the faithful: "[T]his is . . . one of the precious exceedingly great promises granted unto us poor miserable sinners, that we through them should become partakers of the divine nature, and should be so highly honored as not only to be loved by God through Christ Jesus . . . but should even have the Lord himself dwelling completely in us."[7] "'Filled unto all the fullness of God' means . . . full of God, adorned with his grace and the gifts of his Spirit—the Spirit who gives us steadfastness, illuminates us with his light, lives within us his life, saves us with his salvation, and enkindles love in us; . . . it means having God and all his blessings dwelling in us in fullness and being effective to make us wholly divine . . ."[8] Regarding one in whom God dwells, Luther says: He "makes daily progress in life and good works . . . , is useful to God and man; through him . . . men and countries receive benefit . . . ; and such a man's words, life and doings are God's."[9] "Christians are indeed called and made the habitation of God, and in them God speaks and rules and works."[10] "For through faith Christ is in us, indeed, one with us."[11] Through Christ's love, "we are to be changed and to make the infirmities of all other Christians our own; we are to take upon ourselves their form and their necessity, and all the good that is within our power we are to make theirs, that they may profit from it . . . [W]e are changed into one another and are made into a community by love."[12]

No obstacle faced by the church in living its public vocation, indeed no power in heaven and earth, is greater than the living Christ within, with, and under all things, and in a particular way dwelling within the assembly of believers, the public church. For Luther, it is as abode of Christ that the assembly of the faithful becomes Christ to all, proclaiming the good news, sharing Word and Supper, seeking the well-being of others, striving for justice and peace, and not fleeing the suffering that may result from these commitments. "Christ who lives in me" *is* the love that loves neighbor. Christ is not only object of faith, but also active agent of it.

According to Luther, Christ's love has two dimensions: "The love Christ bears toward us, and the love we owe our neighbor."[13] In a sermon written five years after "The Freedom of a Christian," Luther describes the sequential process whereby we become both "lords of all" and "servants of all." First, through faith, we become "free from sin, alive, saved, and children of God. After [that] . . . we do good and exercise love to our neighbor . . . , become servants of all."[14] Luther explains more fully:

> You see how love makes him a servant, so that he helps the poor man freely and for nothing . . . This is what I often have said, that faith makes of us lord and love makes of us servants. Indeed, by faith we become gods and partakers of the divine nature . . . but through love we become equal to the poorest . . . servants of all. By faith we receive blessings from above, from God; through love we give them out below, to our neighbor.[15]

It is crucial to note that—without exception in Luther's writing—Christ's indwelling is not a consequence of *similitude* between creature and God, but of *dissimilitude,* and is realized not by human effort, but only by God's gift. Herein lies Luther's radical departure from medieval theology. As Reformation historian Stephen Ozment explains, "Luther assailed the fundamental axiom of medieval theology, the conviction that 'likeness' to God is the *sine qua non* for union with God, and hence for salvation."[16] Likeness to God was achievable by human effort and was the indispensable condition for salvation. This principle underlaid monastic practice, mysticism, and the sacramental system of the church. Saving faith was formed by sacramentally infused grace in concert with human effort toward godliness or perfection.[17] Luther absolutely rejected this move toward similitude between creature and Creator on the basis of creaturely effort as a means of salvation.

Bonhoeffer, too, provides Lutheran insights into Christ's indwelling presence as the church's power for public witness. For him, as for Luther, the finite bears the infinite. The "finite" is all of creation. Yet, in a particular way, "the finite" is the church. "Christ's relationship with the church is two-fold; he is the creator of its entire life . . . and he is also really present at all times in his church, for the church is his body . . . In the community, Christ is at work as with an instrument. He is present in it."[18] In Bonhoeffer's terms, Christ dwelling in the church "conforms" it to "the form of Jesus Christ," God's overflowing love incarnate now as a believing community acting responsibly in the world on behalf of abundant life for all and against what thwarts it. That action requires recognizing social evil, naming it, and "putting a spoke in the wheel" of earthly powers that demand disobedience to God. The power to serve others and resist social evil, even when so doing is terribly costly, is the actual love of God as Christ taking form in the community of faith.[19] For Bonhoeffer, as for Luther, the wellspring of the church's power for "participating in God's mission" in the world is the crucified and living Christ abiding in and gradually, but never fully, transforming the community of believers. The church's power is the form of Jesus Christ taking form in and among the people gathered in his name.[20] Christians as objects of Christ's love become subjects of that love. Faith is both "faith in Christ" and "faith of Christ." God, who abides in the church, is a God utterly active in history in every dimension of life, a God drawn to the broken and the bleeding, a God active in public life.

It is an ancient faith claim: that God's love in Christ is "flowing and pouring into all things"[21] and there offers creating, saving, and sustaining power for the healing of a broken world. Incarnate mystery lives in and among us as justice-making, self-honoring neighbor-love. This church may be called to rekindle that ancient faith claim, to breathe and live in the promise that God is incarnate in us—mud creatures of the earth, gathered to praise God and "participate in God's mission"—and, in us, is hungering and hastening toward the restoration of this precious and brutalized world. This vision breathes power to open our hearts and minds to the "data of despair" and not drown in it, but rather enter into it on behalf of life abundant for all. Thus speaks the incarnation today. In the face of hopelessness or despair, herein lies hope and power for living as body of Christ.

"The Holy Spirit Streams into the Heart"

One synodical bishop, when asked what was needed personally to be more active in bold public witness, responded with humble honesty: "courage." When questioned how one builds courage for public witness, the bishop responded, "On this subject I do not yet know . . . but I would like to learn." Some forms of public witness require the courage to face disapproval or conflict and respond to it faithfully and fruitfully. Public witness may, in fact, be dangerous, even life-threatening, calling for courage beyond what we believe we have. This should come as no surprise to a people who publicly has vowed to "renounce all the forces of evil."[22]

Luther was convinced that the Holy Spirit imparts courage, strength, and power to those who believe. Christians, he writes, are "far more powerful through the Holy Spirit, and are undaunted by the world, the devil, death, and all kinds of misfortune . . . The Hebrew word 'spirit' might well be rendered '*bold, undaunted courage*'"[23] (italics mine). Luther's words invite this public church to accept ever more fully the Holy Spirit in our midst, bringing courage for faith active in love. He writes [gender-neutral language substituted],

- "This is the Holy Spirit's office: to rule inwardly in the heart, making "it burn and create new courage so that a [person] grows happy before God . . . and with a happy heart serves the people."[24]
- "[T]he Holy Spirit inspires new thoughts and creates a new mind and heart . . . In addition to the grace by which a [person] begins to believe

and hold fast to the Word, God rules in a [person] through [God's] divine power and agency, so that [she or] he . . . makes daily progress in life and good works . . . , essentially becomes more able to serve [people] and countries in that [her or] his life and doings become God's."[25]

- "The Holy Spirit streams into the heart and makes a new [person], one who loves God and gladly does [God's] will . . . [The Spirit] writes a fiery flame on the heart and makes it alive . . . a new [person] is made who is conscious of a reason, heart, and mind unlike [she or] he formerly had. Everything is now alive . . . [She or] he has . . . a heart which burns with love and delights in whatever pleases God."[26]

- "If we recognize these great gifts, then our hearts will be filled by the Holy Spirit with the love which makes us free, joyful, almighty . . . servants of our neighbors, and yet lords of all."[27]

As we mature as public church, this heritage beckons us to rejoice in, trust, and call upon the courage given in the Spirit for our participation in God's public mission. The ELCA of the 21st century will give thanks for and explore the mystery of being a people "marked with the cross of Christ forever . . . , claimed, gathered, and sent for the sake of the world . . . *by the power of the Holy Spirit* . . ."[28] (italics mine). When the public church is gathered and sent forth for the sake of the world, therein lies power to heed God's call, continuing in the covenant God makes in Holy Baptism.

The Church Is Part of a Larger Dwelling Place of Christ, All That God Created

Luther insists that Christ actually is present not only in believing communities, but in all created things. "Nothing can be more truly present and within all creatures than God himself with his power."[29] "God . . . exists at the same time in every little seed, whole and entire, and yet also in all and above all and outside all created things."[30] "[E]verything is full of Christ through and through . . ."[31] "[A]ll creatures are . . . permeable and present to [Christ]."[32] "Christ . . . fills all things . . . Christ is around us and in us in all places . . . [H]e is present in all creatures, and I might find him in stone, in fire, in water, or even in a rope, for he certainly is there . . ."[33]

While, for Luther, the scope of redemption and of the theo-ethical universe is the human[33]—and these are fault lines with grave consequences[35]— the scope of God's blessed creaturehood *in whom God dwells* and the scope of revelation are cosmic.[36]

The presence of God taking bodily form in "our" many forms suggests a web of connectedness pregnant with implications for the church's moral-spiritual power to live its public vocation. God's earthy and earthly indwelling presence illumines the ELCA's constitutional mandate to "respond to the needs of . . . the whole creation [and] to promote . . . care of the earth,"[37] and our liturgical prayer of dedication to "the care and redemption of all that [God has] made."[38] Luther's witness to God "flowing and pouring into all things"[39] lends provocative theological underpinnings to this dimension of the church's role in public life. The "widespread good" we are to serve is biophysical and geoplanetary. The moral universe expands beyond the human to encompass earth and all of its bounty, not only because God created and cares for them, but also because God "is in and through all creatures, in all their parts and places, so that the world is full of God and He fills all."[40]

Luther's claim that Christ indwells all that God created also beckons us toward less familiar territory. Christ as boundless love—living and loving not only in the assembly of believers, but also in the rest of creation— summons the church to learn ways of hearing and heeding the "witness" of other-than-human creatures and elements. Luther's insistence that "God . . . with his power is present in every single creature"[41] hints at a dimension of moral-spiritual power for living into our calling, a dimension little probed in modern theological discourse. If God dwells in "all created things," then in what sense does or might God's presence and power there nurture human agency to participate in God's work in the world? If "Christ . . . is present in all creatures, and I might find him in stone, in fire, in water . . . for he certainly is there . . . ,"[42] then is it possible that creating, redeeming, and sustaining love lives in the creatures and elements of God's creation? Could it be that the cosmos embodies God not only as creative and revelatory presence, but also as teaching, saving, and sustaining presence that could nourish the church for its public vocation?

Unfolding those possibilities is beyond the scope of this project. Suffice it to say that Luther's sense of God indwelling all created things opens that door theologically. Exploring the expansive, fertile terrain on the other side may be a vital contribution of this church to what Thomas Berry calls the "great work"[43] before humankind in our day: moving the human species into a sustainable relationship with our planetary home.

Cross and Resurrection Bear Hope

Where God seems hidden, there God is. This inquiry has embraced the promise that this church is a people of the incarnate God. However, a church of the incarnation is not a church of Jesus Christ unless that incarnation includes the crucifixion and resurrection. This is the centerpiece of Lutheran theology. As a people of the incarnation, we are a community given life by the cross and resurrection of Christ.

We spoke above of the despair or hopelessness that even people of good faith may feel regarding social brokenness. Widespread hopelessness is an ominous social illness and can lead to alienation from God. Indeed, the evidence of the 20th century lures the aware toward despair. To social pain has been added ecological suffering.

- The gap between rich and poor is widening. According to a United Nations report, "New estimates show that the 225 richest people have combined wealth equal to the annual income of the poorest 47 percent of the world's people."[44] For the most impoverished, "poverty means death."[45]
- A 1992 "Warning to Humanity" issued by more than 1600 senior scientists, including a majority of all living Nobel Laureates in the sciences, advises, "Human beings and the natural world [sic] are on a collision course . . . [that] may so alter the living world that it will be unable to sustain life in the manner that we know."[46]

Hopelessness drains the power to act for the sake of the world.

In the face of despair in its many forms, the cross and resurrection bring hope and with it the power born of hope. Despair has many faces.

For some people, despair is born of fear that God must be absent, given the immensity of human brokenness and suffering. Amidst this form of hopelessness, the cross of Christ is perhaps most life-giving. The cross attests that the only power which truly can heal creation is *drawn instinctively there, to suffering and brokenness,* and there is most fully known.[47] God's works are hidden in the form of their opposite (*sub contrario suo abscondita sunt*). God is present in—rather than absent from—agony. However, when we cry out over the tortured brokenness of life for so many or in the midst of our own suffering, we need more than a God who is present and revealed. We hunger for a God who is with us *on behalf of us,* intimately intertwined with us, embracing and suffering with us. This is the yet deeper truth of the cross. God is not only present and known in brokenness; God also is present there *for us,* participating in our very being, and bringing healing and life in times and ways that we cannot fully comprehend. This is a fundamental faith claim for a people of the cross.[48]

For other people, despair is sown by a deep sense that things indeed *will* continue as they are in this world. Christ crucified and risen promises otherwise. Nothing in all of creation finally can separate this splendid and broken creation "from the love of God in Christ Jesus" (Romans 8:39). We have been told the end of the story, and it is resurrection. In the midst of suffering and death—be it individual, social, or ecological—the promise given to the Earth community is that life in God will reign. God in Christ is restoring the Earth community and will redeem human beings from living as its enemies. God's future for creation is life abundant for all. So speaks the resurrection.

Hopelessness grows too from the dread that we have not the courage to follow God's call. The risks and dangers involved in serving a God of justice-making love in a world of injustice and violence are too great. It is a reasonable fear for a people of the cross. According to the Gospel as told by Mark, Jesus said, "Take up your cross and follow me" (8:34), *after* he already had been marked by the powers-that-be as a danger to their power and to the reigning political, religious, cultural, and economic power alignments. Jesus apparently was aware of the powers lined up against him when he called his disciples to "follow me." Furthermore, he was resolutely on "the way"[49] to the seat of power for a final confrontation that would end with his execution as a threat to entrenched powers. As Jesuit priest Phillip

Berrigan has commented, if you want to follow Jesus, "you had better look good on wood." Our Lutheran brothers and sisters in El Salvador, Jerusalem, South Africa, and elsewhere have lived the truth of this claim. This faith community, the ELCA, claims as central to its being and purpose an "execution stake."[50] What happens when one who was executed for his faithfulness to God says, "take up your cross and follow me," and says it while he is on "the way" to that execution. What happens when we hear this call? It would seem that denial of the call and fear of its implications would keep us from following, render us powerless. Indeed it may. However, the cross speaks otherwise: in coming face to face with our fear, we encounter the grace of God. In receiving that grace, we know God who abides in and among us. What happens when God "abides in" a community created to participate in God's mission on earth, and abiding there draws forth power we feared we did not have? God is present in life's broken and bleeding places, including our fear. God can be trusted to restore God's good creation, in spite of all forces that would foil it. Thus says the resurrection. Thus speaks Easter.

True hope is not born of closing hearts and minds to the "data of despair." Indeed, Christ crucified impels us to suspect theological claims that "do not take seriously the suffering in the world."[51] In Christ crucified and risen, God offers, and thus *this public church must proclaim to the world,* true hope in the face of widespread, yet subtle, despair. A theology of the cross and resurrection is a theology of hope. A people of the cross and resurrection is a bearer of hope, hope active in love. It is our God-given responsibility as public church to keep alive in public the good news that

- God's love for each person and for this world is boundless and never will be stopped by any force in earth or heaven;
- God is present where God seems absent, even in the midst of agony and the apparent triumph of evil;
- God is restoring creation from all that would destroy the abundant life for all that God has given; and
- God will redeem human beings from living in enmity with earth's web of life.

In this hope is power to heed the covenant God makes with us in baptism, power to be public church in public life.

The power that frees and sends the church is God's power, given in Christ and Spirit so that we might serve God's mission. How God bestows this gift is mystery. We put reason and words to this mystery, so that glimpsing it less dimly, we might receive it more fully. Here we have explored, not definitively but suggestively, a few dimensions of that gift as expressed by Martin Luther: Christ abiding in and among the assembly of believers gathered in Christ's name, the Holy Spirit pouring into us, Christ filling all things, and the power of hope born of cross and resurrection.

⤠

We have sketched the contours of this public church and its vocation by journeying through the marks of the baptized. We have named formidable obstacles to living out that vocation as public church in public life, and we have pointed the way to wellsprings of power for so living in spite of those deterrents. This public church, a people "marked with the cross of Christ forever,"[52] is a *people of the incarnation—cross, resurrection, and living presence—as a way of living in and for the world.* A Lutheran theology of the cross held inseparably with a theology of the resurrection and of Christ filling all things offers to the church hope, courage, and guidance for living out our baptismal vocation in public life. Jesus Christ beckons us to trust a God who is drawn to life's broken places and there draws forth healing power, to a God who is more powerful as love embodied than any force in heaven or earth, including death itself, and to a God who is "flowing and pouring into all things."[53] To be public church, with all of our flaws and failures, is to be a beloved assembly of baptized believers created, claimed, gathered, and sent by God to serve God's mission. We give thanks for, witness to, and participate in God's work in the world.

In what ways, then, are we to live as a people of the incarnation on this generous and tormented planet today? How does the ELCA live into who we are in the midst of public powers of violence, brokenness, and exploitation in our day? These are primary questions for this community of the cross, resurrection, and living presence of Jesus Christ.

Questions for Reflection

1. What in your faith inspires, motivates, or empowers you to "seek justice and peace in all the earth"?

2. What gives you the courage to renounce the forces of evil in this world?

3. What difference does the presence of Christ in "the other" make in the way that you relate with others? What difference does the presence of Christ in you and in the faith community make in your ways of relating with others and with yourself? What difference does Christ "filling all things [even the tiniest leaf]" make in the ways you related with self, others, the earth, and God?

4. What spiritual resources provoke within you and evoke from you the responses of love for neighbor and care and redemption of all creation?

5. What role does the community of Christ play in your faithful witness to the love of God as revealed in Jesus?

5

People of the Incarnation
As a Way of Living

This public church is a people of the cross, resurrection, and living presence of Jesus Christ. What shape does that "way of living" take, for the ELCA, at the dawn of the 21st century? How are congregations, synods, units of the church-wide organization, ordained ministers, baptized members, bishops, and presiding bishop to be a people of the incarnation, a people of Christ's cross, resurrection, and living presence? How are we to give social form to what God is doing in and for this world?

The greatest value of these questions is in the asking and re-asking of them, and in the guidance of partial responses. For the "answers" cannot be definitive, final, or certain. True to a Lutheran theological method, they must be contextual, born of particular people's lives, suffering, and struggles.

Guideposts for the Way

A few things are foundational and provide guideposts into this terrain:

- *The heart of this public church's lifework will be worship that is centered in God's grace in Jesus Christ,* received in the Word proclaimed, the waters of Baptism, and the bread and wine.
- *The marks of the baptized will be the contours of the church's life.* The ELCA exists in many and tremendously varied contexts. Jesus addressed particular forms of alienation from God in each town and countryside and in the cultural ethos and political economy of which he was a self-conscious and critical part. Likewise, Luther and the confessors spoke directly to the distinct realities of life in particular situations and their broader context.

- *Assemblies in this heritage will address the specific forms of alienation from God that characterize our many particular contexts.*
- *Marked by the cross of Christ forever, this church will assume that proclaiming and giving social form to God's ways will be life-giving, and may be dangerous and costly.*
- *This faith community will keep alive in public the good news and the hope that it bears.*

These, then, are guideposts for our way of living as public church. The remainder of this inquiry presupposes them and is informed by them.

The vocation of this public church is, ecumenically and globally, to praise God for God's work in the world, "tell the story of it," and be God's "rusty tools" in it. The aspects of this lifework are, of course, manifold! The ELCA is experienced and apt in many of these aspects. They include worship centered in the means of grace, catechesis, ongoing Christian education, social ministries, public policy advocacy, community-based organizing, and more. We affirm, give thanks for, and support these. And we are to continue shaping and recreating them in light of changing circumstances and the church's maturing understanding of its being, vision, and mission. Interrelating these pieces of our work so that they nurture and inform each other ever more richly may be a primary task of this public church today and for the foreseeable future, and will give shape to our life together.

Other dimensions of this lifework, less familiar in this church, may be called forth by current socioecological realities, the ongoing maturing of the church, or the whispering of the Holy Spirit. Identifying these myriad dimensions exceeds the scope of this book. The remainder of this discussion simply explores three dimensions for which our society stands in great need, and for which the Lutheran tradition is theologically and ecclesiologically well gifted. They are dimensions of witness that require careful and prayerful attention, for they are potentially divisive. In light of that, the first of the three is a necessary precedent to the other two. Shaped by the marks of the baptized and by a Lutheran heritage, this church is well suited to provide

- public leadership in moral discernment;
- leadership in public lament; and

• public leadership in critique of and resistance to societal wrong, and in the quest for more just, compassionate, and sustainable ways of living.

Public Leadership in Moral Discernment

We are to seek signs of God working amidst the beauty, confusion, and wreckage of history, so that we may praise God for that work, witness to it, and be "the hands, channels, and means through which God" works.[1] *Have mercy on us, Lord, but so often we do not know what you are doing in the world! How, then, can we participate in it and witness to it?* The church is called to ongoing discernment. Amidst the complexity and moral ambiguity of life, *how* are we to discern what God is doing in any given situation, and how might we most faithfully give social form to God's work? In both interpersonal and international venues how are we to discern what God is doing, so that we may align ourselves with it? The volumes probing this question could fill libraries; what more can be said from the particularity of this church in this time?

Lutheran theology offers invaluable clues. It assures us that human beings *cannot know with certainty* what God is doing in the world; yet, paradoxically and in the face of uncertainty, we are to act in accord with God's mission and activity as we understand it through faithful discernment. Said differently, we disbelieve any claim to absolute knowledge of God's ways or will, as well as any claim that God's people are, therefore, excused from seeking to live in congruence with it.

The next clue is unsettling, perhaps unwelcome. From a Lutheran theological perspective, knowledge of how we are to live is inseparable from knowing God ("knowing" here refers less to "knowledge of" than to "being in relationship with"[2]). A Lutheran theology of the cross counsels that the work and ways of God are revealed most fully in Jesus Christ, and—in some way beyond full human comprehension—that this one is known most deeply in brokenness and suffering. Thus, we will glimpse what God is doing, to the extent that we allow ourselves to be present in profound solidarity[3] and compassion where people and creation suffer most.

A Lutheran ethical approach suggests that our response to any given situation is more likely to cohere with God's work if that response is guided by a framing question and four overarching norms. The question is, How are we to perceive this situation and respond to it *because of* God's boundless love for creation and presence with, in, and for it, especially as seen in Jesus Christ, witnessed to by communities of believers throughout time, and experienced yet today in the Spirit. The four broad norms are

- receiving and trusting the gracious love of God;
- loving God with heart, soul, mind, and strength;
- loving "neighbor" with self-honoring and justice-making love; and
- living toward sustainable Earth-human relations.

The ways of God are more likely to be reflected in what enables these norms than in what contradicts them. For Lutherans, responding to this framing question and discerning ways of doing and being consistent with these norms is not the work of solitary individuals. A Lutheran ecclesiology locates that discernment as the work of the church, be it in small circles, congregations, synods, or the church-wide organization.

Christian discernment that seeks to cohere with God's mission in matters of public life is not primarily a specific task or moment. It has more to do with how we see and know in everyday life, as that seeing and knowing that develop over a lifetime and throughout the ages of the church. Discernment is the disciplined art of coming to know ever more fully the mystery that is God, coming to see ever more clearly the historical realities of life on earth, and holding these two in one breath, so that we may come closer to knowing where God is at work in these earthly realities.

"Seeing realities of life on earth" refers to perceiving "what *is* going on"—including historical roots and likely consequences—and "what *could be* going on," that is, alternatives. The heart of discernment is to hold "what is" and "what could be" in light of the life-giving, life-saving, life-sustaining mystery of God's ongoing work toward the redemption and flourishing of creation. Said differently, we are to hold our earthly realities in one breath with the power and presence of God, in order to craft ways of living that proclaim God as seen in Jesus Christ. Where vision of life's realities is obscured by illusions, a task of Christian discernment is *to see* differently, so that we might *live* differently. Where dominant forces distort historical realities by describing them falsely, Christian discernment must re-see and then "re-describe the world."[4]

This emphasis on "seeing" reflects a sense that crucial moral weight lies in perceptions of what *is*. *What* we see and refuse to see, and *how* we see, are morally significant, bearing on whether we foster life-giving ways or thwart them. When well-intentioned people blindly accept situations or beliefs as natural, inevitable, or divinely ordained when they are not, we perpetuate those situations or beliefs. The uncritical acceptance of comfortable illusions regarding social or ecological realities that damage neighbors far and near leads to faulty discernment and complicity with that damage. Morally responsible sight is a moral imperative of faith and a necessary ingredient of discernment.

How is the church to "see" ever more clearly? How are we, as part of everyday faith life, to nurture critical vision? What enables morally responsible seeing, especially seeing the power arrangements that determine who has the necessities for life with dignity and the terms of humankind's relationship to the planet?

A theology of the cross tenders a clue. In Bonhoeffer's words, seeing "from below, from the perspective of the outcast, the suspects, the maltreated, the powerless, the oppressed, the reviled—in short, from the perspective of those who suffer" is "an experience of incomparable worth."[5] For Christians in positions of "privilege," moral discernment is fatally flawed if it does not begin with—and otherwise heed—the cries, claims, and constructive proposals of those on the "margins" of society, especially people whose survival, dignity, or human rights are at risk in whatever situation is at hand. ("Privilege" here means having advantages by virtue of the social category to which one belongs. Those categories may be determined by race/ethnicity, economic status, gender, sexual orientation, etc.) Privilege filters all that we see, protecting us from seeing reality through the eyes of those whose misery may be caused by our privilege. We then make moral decisions and indeed structure society around what is good for us, thinking, in oblivious innocence, that it is good for all. Theologically, to ignore or minimize the voices of those on the underside of history contradicts what we know of God in Jesus. The arts of critical vision and thus of faithful moral discernment, practiced by this church, would include asking,

What are the lenses through which we are seeing? Whose voices and knowledge are heard, and whose are erased in deliberations within the church and in the dominant public discourse? Who is absent from the table of deliberation?

In this, the ELCA is gifted. We are composed of people on the margins and people at the centers of power. Some of us, in fact, inhabit both. This church recognizes the deep need to be more diverse, and is becoming better at enabling all to be heeded. And we are able to "see" through the multivalent lenses of a communion of Lutheran churches worldwide, a communion that includes people who have been cast to the edges. In many ways this church has sought to hear their voices.[6] Today, in order to discern how God is at work in the world, this public church is challenged to create channels for hearing ever more fully the voices of people—within the Lutheran communion and from without—on the underside of power and privilege.

A church committed to discerning where God seems to be at work and developing tools for that process, may be a church well equipped to provide space and leadership for the broader public to wrestle with ambiguous moral issues. Conundrums emerge: does convening tables for deliberative moral discourse preclude taking a moral stand at them? If so, which is a more crucial public role of the church? What "language" are we to speak? Providing leadership in public moral discernment might invite this church to cultivate competence in speaking four "dialects"—for conversation within the Lutheran communion, within the broader Christian community, with other faith traditions, and with people outside of faith traditions who are seeking moral wisdom.

Leadership in Public Lament

The church is called to seek social healing. This church responds to that call with ardor and sensitivity, recalling—especially in worship—that gratitude to God is integral to wholeness and healing. In liturgy and in prayer we give thanks. Our life as a public church centers around a great thanksgiving. One role of this church is to "return thanks" to the Giver of all good, inviting others to that centerpiece of life.

Gratitude, as an element of healing, has a less recognized sister. Christian ethicist Emilie Townes names it. In a powerful sermon on the book of Joel, she claims that, for people living in covenant relationship with God, social healing begins with communal lament:

> If we learn anything from Joel
> it is to know that the healing of brokenness and injustice
> the healing of social sin and degradation
> the healing of spiritual doubts and fears
> begins with an unrestrained lament . . .
> It's a lament of faith
> to the God of faith
> that we need help
> that we can't do this ministry alone
> we can't witness to the world in isolation
> we can't fight off the hordes of wickedness and hatred with a big
> stick
> we can't do this by ourselves anymore, God
> we need . . . divine help.[7]

Lament was integral to the ancient Hebrews' covenant relationship with God, suggests Townes, drawing on the work of Walter Brueggemann. A loss of lament meant "also a loss of genuine covenant interaction with God."[8] Where the assembly praises God but does not lament, "covenant is a practice of denial and pretense."[9]

Communal lament, as Townes explains it, is the assembly crying out in distress to the God in whom it trusts. It is a cry of sorrow by the people gathered, a cry of grief and repentance and a plea for help in the midst of social affliction. Deep and sincere "communal lament . . . names problems, seeks justice, and hopes for God's deliverance. Lament, as seen in the book of Joel, she says, *forms* people; it requires them to give name and words to suffering. [W]hen Israel used lament as rite and worship on a regular basis, it kept the question of justice visible and legitimate."[10]

Could it be that communal lament is a key to social healing in the publics in which this church is called to minister? Who is more suited to lament and call forth public lament than a people of the cross, a people called to be present where life is broken, where people suffer, where the earth groans? Who is more equipped to face and lament social agony—rather than deny it—than a people who knows that ultimately the power of God's love will reign? Who is better formed for lament than a people who claims trust in God above all else as the essence of faith, and who, in that trust, is called to "serve all people, following the example of our Lord Jesus?" When and how might worship be the public processing of grief and pain regarding societal, ecological, and individual brokenness? When and how might this public church open doors to public lament?

Public Leadership in Resistance and the Quest for Just and Sustainable Ways of Living

We are public church in an earth community of magnificent beauty, goodness, and joy, yet wracked with suffering. Suffering is a multi-valent concept. It covers both suffering that is natural and inevitable, and suffering that is caused by human decisions and actions. In some humanly caused suffering, "we" or "I" may be implicated, and in other cases, "we" or "I" may be innocent (in reality, of course, these distinctions usually overlap and intertwine). A faithful response to one form of suffering may differ from a faithful response to another. Neighbor-love takes distinctive forms in the face of each. Where suffering is humanly caused, faith active in love may seek to accompany and comfort, as well as to intervene in the cause of the suffering. That intervention takes varied forms, from mending broken interpersonal relationships to seeking change in public policy and social structures. This church is deeply involved in many types of work to address causes of unnecessary suffering. Here we consider one form of that work: critique and resistance.

Where people recognize social structural sin, refuse to be silent in the face of it, refrain (to the extent possible) from participation in it, and seek more just and compassionate alternatives, resistance is at work. Where it is a response to God's love known in Christ and is guided by the Holy Spirit, it is Christian resistance, an act of evangelical defiance. This is a powerful form of Christian witness. It attests to faith that no power of wrong will prevail over the justice-making, earth-treasuring love of God for this world, in spite of appearances to the contrary. Evangelical defiance declares in faith that no political, economic, or cultural trend that contradicts God's saving purpose is inevitable, even if it seems to be so. Herein lies a center-piece of evangelical defiance. Tremendous moral deception and wrong are perpetrated when humanly constructed belief systems, social structures, or power arrangements are claimed as natural, inevitable, or divinely ordained. Throughout history, those designations have rationalized or justified injustice and other forms of cruelty. A crucial role of Christian resistance is to expose and dismantle false claims to divine blessing or to inevitability grounded in divine mandate. Resistance is integral to life with God for a people who pledge in baptism "to renounce all the forces of evil, the devil, and all his empty promises."[11]

Faith-based resistance is fraught with ambiguity and born of repentance and humility. It entails taking a stand in a world where moral certainty often is impossible and human efforts toward the good are intermingled with sin, where self-righteousness rears its head in the midst of self-giving actions and the pull to equate one's course to the will of God is almost magnetic. Thus Christian resistance, and in particular Lutheran Christian resistance, is housed in a conviction that the hopes of the resisters, the alternatives toward which they point or the policies they promote, are *not* the gospel of Christ or the reign of God. These efforts and visions—honest and noble as they may be—are fallible human attempts to know and approximate ways of living consistent with the God revealed in Jesus Christ. In emphasizing this conviction, even insisting upon it, Lutheran Christian resistance offers invaluable service to the broader public.

The Christian tradition is richly rooted in informed and vehement critique of and resistance to decisions and actions by the powerful where they thwart God's gifts of peace, justice, and flourishing of the *oikos* ("the entirety of God's created household"). Prophetic critique and denunciation are at the core of who we are. We are descendants of resisters: the Hebrew prophets, Jesus, the early church martyrs, medieval mystics who dared to know God beyond the ways of knowing dictated by church hierarchy, Martin Luther and the confessors, the resisting church under Nazi rule, the civil rights movement, the resisting church of South Africa, and on and on.

Evangelical critique and resistance begin with compassion and discernment and the latter's call to critical seeing. From there, critique and resistance take myriad forms, depending upon the situation and the gifts of the people involved: prayer; fasting; public speaking; worship; prayerful vigils; public celebration; civil disobedience; educational outreach; dialogue in neighborhoods and congregations; legislative and electoral advocacy; public protest; theater, art, music, poetry; consumer advocacy through boycotts, shareholder actions, and socially responsible purchasing and investing; and more. The forms are as rich as the creative vision of people who, seeing societal wrong, are led to critique and resist it for the sake of a more just, compassionate, and peaceful world.

How might this public church honor the call to faith-based resistance as act of neighbor-love? How are we to form ourselves—corporately—for evangelical defiance where it is called for? Biblical scholar Wayne Meeks suggests that what set Christian morality apart from other moral discourses of late antiquity was "the creation of this peculiar story in which each [one] is called on to be a character, and from which character itself and virtue take their meaning."[12] Recent narrative theologians and philosophers concur: the stories in which we situate ourselves form moral vision and agency. *Weapons of the Spirit* is the story in film of a Huguenot village in occupied France in which villagers, led by the Protestant pastor and teacher, resisted the mandate to turn in Jews and instead rescued nearly 4,000 Jewish people at the risk of torture or death. "What," asks the viewer, "enabled these everyday Christians to resist social evil?" As the film unfolds, one finds a key. The church of this village located itself explicitly in a narrative of Christian resisters, most notably the story of its Huguenot forebears. The people told and retold that narrative in song, story, and sermon. In the face of ever-present but less evident forms of social sin today, could it be that this church is to teach our people, young and old, the narratives of resistance in which we identify with faith forebears whose faith in God enabled them to resist social structural evil despite the risks?

Where Christians are called to critique and resist social evil, they are called to seek and embrace more just, compassionate, and sustainable alternatives. That quest, the partner of resistance, has been present in the ELCA's story since its earliest chapters in the lives of the ancient Hebrews in relationship with the God whom Jesus loved. May we, encouraged and inspired by the witness of our faith ancestors and of sisters and brothers today, carry on that quest.

What is the shape of life for a people of the incarnation—the body of the crucified, risen, and living God—in the publics in which this church is called to praise and serve God today? After noting a few firm guidelines and affirming ways that this church already gives social form to our understanding of God's work in the world, we sketched additional complementary possibilities. They are dimensions of living, dying, and rising as public church that could meet deep needs in our society by drawing upon gifts of the Lutheran tradition.

Questions for Reflection

1. As you examine this world in which we live, about what do you lament as a sign of compassion and of hunger for a more just, compassionate, and ecologically sustainable world?

2. When and how might worship in your congregation be a place for public "lament" regarding societal, ecological, and individual brokenness?

3. Re-read the paragraphs on "seeing" on pages 65-67. What comes to mind when you read them? Discuss concrete examples of "situations or beliefs that well-intentioned people blindly accept as normal, natural, inevitable, or divinely ordained." Discuss concrete examples of "uncritical acceptance of comfortable illusions regarding social or ecological realities that may be damaging to neighbors far or near." What do you think of the notion that we have a moral obligation to see clearly?

4. Do you think that Jesus offered evangelical defiance? If so, to what? What can we learn from the life of Jesus about faith-based critique and resistance?

5. Page 71 suggests that "evangelical critique and resistance begin with compassion and discernment," from there taking many different forms depending upon the situation and the gifts of the people involved. Discuss a time when you or your faith community or another part of the Christian community has offered faith-based critique and resistance. What form did those offerings take?

6. Discuss a time in which you or your faith community or another part of the Christian community provided leadership in "the quest for more just, compassionate, and sustainable ways of living." What was the impact on your relationships with other people? On your relationship with God? On your sense of hope?

7. Where do you find hope in the face of evil that is done in the sight of God?

Closing

What does it mean for the Evangelical Lutheran Church in America to be a public church with a public vocation today? This inquiry has unfolded in challenge, paradox, and hope. We first sketched the contours of this public church and its vocation by remembering our baptismal vows. We then named formidable obstacles to living out that vocation, and wellsprings of power for doing so in spite of those deterrents. Together these inquiries led to a vision of this church as a community of the incarnation, where incarnation means Jesus's life, crucifixion, and resurrection, and the living presence of Christ with, in, and among us today. Finally, we began to explore the shape of everyday life for people of the incarnation as a "way of living" in public. For followers of Jesus, that "way of living"—in a world of breathtaking splendor, yet where evil often parades as good—is dangerous and costly and gives life abundant, now and forever. That "way of living" is a gift from God to this church, "a people created by God in Christ, empowered by the Holy Spirit, called and sent to bear witness to God's creative, redeeming, and sanctifying activity in the world . . . to participate in God's mission . . ."[1] May this inquisitive and suggestive journey catalyze further inquiry into the mystery and shape of life as God's public church in public life today, "marked with the cross of Christ forever . . . , claimed, gathered, and sent for the sake of the world."[2]

Questions for Reflection

1. What do you understand to be the church's vocation in public life? What does it mean to you to be part of a public church with a public vocation in the world today? What do you think it means for your congregation?

2. What are the implications for you of being part of a "people of the incarnation where incarnation means Jesus's life, crucifixion, and resurrection, and the living presence of Christ with, in, and among us today"?

3. What additional questions are raised for you by this book?

4. Where does this study lead you? Where does it lead your congregation? Where does it lead the broader church?

Notes

Introduction

1. From *Lutheran Book of Worship* (*LBW;* Minneapolis: Augsburg Publishing House, and Philadelphia: Board of Publication, Lutheran Church in America, 1978), 201.
2. *Constitutions, Bylaws, and Continuing Resolutions of the Evangelical Lutheran Church in America* (1987), 7.31.12.
3. Evangelical Lutheran Church in America, "The Use of the Means of Grace: A Statement on the Practice of Word and Sacrament" (1997), 12.
4. *LBW,* 81.
5. *LBW,* 124.
6. As in the *Constitutions,* "this church" hereafter in this essay refers to the ELCA. See *Constitutions* 1.02.
7. One of five strategic directions in "Faithful Yet Changing: The Plan for Mission in the Evangelical Lutheran Church in America" (2003).

Chapter 1

1. See Wayne A. Meeks, *The Origins of Christian Morality: The First Two Centuries* (New Haven: Yale University Press, 1993).
2. Martin Luther, *D. Martin Luthers Werke: Kritische Gesamtausgabe* (Weimar: Böhlau, 1883), known as the *Weimar Ausgabe* (*WA*), 2.413.27, cited by George W. Forell, *Faith Active in Love* (Minneapolis: Augsburg Publishing House, 1954), 92.
3. As cited by Mary Solberg in *Compelling Knowledge: A Feminist Proposal for an Epistemology of the Cross* (Albany: SUNY Press, 1997).
4. This is articulated well in the ELCA social statement "The Church in Society" (Chicago: ELCA, 1991), 2.
5. This dynamic is noted by Rasmussen, "Community of the Cross," *Dialog* 30, no. 2 (1991): 162.
6. Heinrich Bornkamm explains that at least two dialectical pairs appear in Luther's thought: the relationship between "proclamation

and lawmaking" on the one hand, and on the other "the two sets of relationships within which the Christian lives," each with a corresponding mode of governance, the Word of God and temporal government. Luther, however, expresses these with multiple terms: "kingdom of God/worldly kingdom, gospel/law, the faithful/the infidels, spiritual/secular, for one's self/for others, the Word of God/the sword, and so forth . . ." See Heinrich Bornkamm, *Luther's Doctrine of the Two Kingdoms* (Philadelphia: Fortress, 1966), 8-9. Interpreters have employed these terms: spiritual/temporal modes of governance, redemption/creation; the church's gospel witness/its ethical witness; sin, death, evil/faith, hope, love; law/gospel; secular world/world of church; kingdom of God/kingdom of the devil; and more. The confusion "stems from two different theological models that are unevenly blended in Luther's own theology . . ." Vitor Westhelle, "The Word and the Mask," draft of unpublished paper. While most scholars indeed find two distinct yet related basic dialectics, others find three. Thus, the complexity thickens.

7. Bornkamm, 2.

8. In the *Constitutions* of the ELCA, the word first appears as an adjective modifying "worship": "public worship."

9. Ronald F. Thiemann, *Religion and Public Life: A Dilemma for Democracy* (Washington, D.C.: Georgetown, 1996), 152. More recently, "public," especially in international NGO discourse, has connoted "civil society," all aspects of society not of government or private. This, too, truncates the term's significance.

10. Iris Marion Young, *Democracy and Inclusion* (New York: Oxford University Press, 2000), 119.

11. Linell E. Cady, "The Intellectual and Effective Critique," *CSSR Bulletin* 27 (April 1998): 36.

12. Larry Rasmussen, "A Different Discipline," *Union Seminary Quarterly Review* 53, no. 3–4 (1999): 38.

13. This is John Howard Yoder's critique of H. Richard Niebuhr's classic and influential distinction between church and culture. See Glen M. Stassen, D. M. Yeager, and John Howard Yoder, *Authentic Transformation* (Nashville: Abingdon, 1996), 31-90.

14. Larry Rasmussen, "A Community of the Cross,"28.
15. "Faithful Yet Changing," mission statement.
16. "When something has a price and is bought and sold, it becomes a commodity....One tendency in a capitalist society is for more aspects of life to be reduced to commodities over time." Pamela Sparr, "United Methodist Study Guide on Global Economics: Seeking a Christian Ethics" (General Board of Global Ministries, United Methodist Church, 1993), 15.
17. The key rationales undergirding this trend revolve around efficiency and growth. Privatization, it is argued, generates economic growth directly, as well as indirectly by increasing competition which increases efficiency. Increased efficiency lowers consumer prices and generates further growth. Growth increases prosperity, employment, consumption, and living standards, ultimately benefiting all. Most economic and other social problems are best solved by means of the unrestricted market processes. (The exception is problems arising from external shocks such as natural disasters and war.) In sum, commodification and privatization contribute to growth which benefits all. I address this argument more fully in Cynthia Moe-Lobeda, *Healing a Broken World: Globalization and God* (Minneapolis: Fortress Press, 2002), chapters 1 and 3.
18. To illustrate, as health care in the United States is increasingly privatized, what happens to those who need expensive medication for severe mental illness or chronic mental or physical disease, but cannot afford its market cost?
19. UNDP, *United Nations Human Development Report 1999* (New York: Oxford University Press, 1999), 67.
20. See, for example, David Hollenbach, SJ, *The Common Good and Christian Ethics* Cambridge: Cambridge University Press, 2002).
21. Ibid., 28.
22. Ibid., 10.
23. Ibid., 3.
24. Thus the claim of some Christians to disavow politics for an apolitical faith life is misguided. Social life is political; apparent non-participation in political processes constitutes a political stand for whatever "the

winners" advocate. Joseph Allen in *Love and Conflict: A Covenantal Model of Christian Ethics* (Nashville: Abingdon, 1984) argues this point well. He rightly points out also that the empirical and normative relationship of religion to the political, and of faith life to political life, has been understood in highly divergent ways throughout history by theologians and political philosophers. Perspectives range from Aristotle's notion that humans are political by nature, to the Augustinian notion that the political is a divine remedy for human sinfulness, to the classic liberal notion of society as a realm of peoples' "individual activity which precedes politics and is apolitical . . . [and upon which] politics and political institutions intrude" (255).

25. Irenaeus of Lyons, *Against Heresies* III.17.3.3.

Chapter 2

1. See, for instance, Affirmation of Baptism (*LBW*), Order of Ordination (*Occasional Services: A Companion to Lutheran Book of Worship* [Minneapolis: Augsburg Publishing House, and Philadelphia: Board of Publication, Lutheran Church in America, 1982]), *Constitutions* of the ELCA, Lutheran confessional writings, and other documents.

2. "[*E*]*kklesia* means 'a people.'" Martin Luther, "On the Councils and the Church," in *Luther's Works* (*LW*), American edition, ed. J. Pelikan and H. Lehmann (Philadelphia: Fortress, 1955), 41:145.

3. *Constitutions,* 4.01-02.

4. *Constitutions,* 2.07.

5. *Constitutions,* 4.02.

6. *LBW,* 121.

7. Ibid., 201.

8. Gordon W. Lathrop, *Holy People: A Liturgical Ecclesiology* (Minneapolis: Augsburg Fortress, 1999), 45.

9. Martin Luther, as cited by Mary Solberg in *Compelling Knowledge.*

10. Martin Luther, as cited by Forell, 92.

11. Martin Luther, "Treatise on Good Works," *LW* 44:52.

12. Martin Luther, "Sermon for the Sixteenth Sunday after Trinity," in John Nicholas Lenker, ed., *Sermons of Martin Luther* (Grand Rapids: Baker Books, 1983), 8:272 (hereafter cited as Lenker). I long have

thought that Luther's sermons ought be taken at least as seriously as his other writings, for he understands the preached word to be the Word of God.

13. Martin Luther, "The Blessed Sacrament of the Holy and True Body and Blood of Christ, and the Brotherhoods," in Timothy F. Lull, ed., *Martin Luther's Basic Theological Works* (Minneapolis: Fortress, 1989), 250.

14. Martin Luther, *LW* 45:172-73.

15. Please note that throughout this book, I have chosen to leave quotations in their original wording, even when it is gender exclusive. The following four statements are from Luther, "The Blessed Sacrament of the Holy and True Body and Blood of Christ, and the Brotherhoods," in Lull, 255, 251, 260, and 250, respectively.

16. See Gordon Lathrop, *Holy Ground: A Liturgical Cosmology* (Minneapolis: Fortress Press, 2003). He artfully insists that liturgies shape and express cosmologies and that those cosmologies in fact form and inform our ways of living in relationship to each other and the earth.

17. For Martin Luther's use of this term and its parallels, see *LW* 10:241 and *LW* 25:291, 313, 345, 351, and 513.

18. Martin Luther, "The Blessed Sacrament of the Holy and True Body and Blood of Christ, and the Brotherhoods," 255.

19. Martin Luther, "Prefaces to the New Testament," *LW* 35:370-71.

20. Ed. Wolfgang Grieve (Geneva: Lutheran World Federation, 2000).

21. "The Use of the Means of Grace," Application 5A.

22. Ibid., Principle 7.

23. Ibid., Application 5A.

24. Ibid.

25. The Rev. Ron Moe-Lobeda, speaking of his experience as a pastor at Luther Place Memorial Church (Washington, D.C.) and its ministry with homeless women.

26. *LBW,* 81.

27. Martin Luther, "The Sacrament of the Body and Blood of Christ— Against the Fanatics," in Lull, 321.

28. Neighbor is a fluid term in Luther's writings, referring variously to all people on Earth, including our enemies, all Christians, and co-residents of a locality.

29. Martin Luther, "The Sacrament of the Body and Blood of Christ—Against the Fanatics," 331.
30. Ibid. Luther also refers to these as Paul's two teachings. See Martin Luther, "Sermon for the Sixteenth Sunday after Trinity," 8:278.
31. Martin Luther, "The Sacrament of the Body and Blood of Christ—Against Fanatics," 331.
32. Martin Luther, "Sermon on the 4th Sunday after Epiphany," in Lenker, 7:69.
33. Martin Luther, "Prefaces to the New Testament," *LW* 35:370. Luther goes on to say: "[This faith] does not ask whether good works are to be done, but before the question is asked, it has already done them and is incessantly doing them."
34. For example, see Martin Luther, "Lectures on Galatians—1535," *LW* 26:127-29.
35. Martin Luther, "Two Kinds of Righteousness," in Lull, 155.
36. Ibid.
37. Ibid., 157.
38. Ibid., 158.
39. Ibid.
40. Martin Luther, "Prefaces to the New Testament," *LW* 35:370.
41. Volumes could be written about the different and conflicting construals of neighbor-love and its moral implications throughout the histories of biblical faith communities.
42. And it does in most dimensions of social life as we know it.
43. The term "pioneering" alternatives is drawn from Diane Yeager in Stassen, Yeager, and Yoder, *Authentic Transformation,* 113-19
44. Walter Brueggemann, "Voices of the Night—Against Justice," in Walter Brueggemann, Thomas H. Groome, and Sharon Parks, *To Act Justly, Love Tenderly, Walk Humbly* (New York: Paulist Press, 1986), writes that doing justice implies "relentless critique of injustice" (7); "envisions a changed social system" (10); and works toward "nothing less than the dismantling of the presently known world for the sake of an alternative world not yet embodied" (11).
45. Christian ethicist Daniel Maguire, in *Moral Core of Judaism and Christianity: Reclaiming the Revolution* (Minneapolis: Fortress, 1993),

affirms that: "In the main biblical perspective, love and justice are not opposites but coordinates, manifestations of the same affect . . . The various words for justice and love in both the Hebrew and Greek scriptures are linguistically interlocking" (220).

46. Commonly held child development theory confirms that humans become able to love by being loved, and that healthy self-love is a requisite of mature capacity to love others. Feminist theory has exposed the damage done to women by the notion that other-love negates self-love, or at least supersedes it morally. For a concise theological critique of the Christian ethical tradition that emphasized other-love to the exclusion of self-love, see Barbara Hilkert Andolsen, "*Agape* in Feminist Ethics," *The Journal of Religious Ethics* 9 (Spring 1981).

47. "An Epistle from the LWF Global Consultation on *Diakonia*" (7 November 2002), 2.

48. See, for example, Martin Luther, "Whether One May Flee from a Deadly Plague," *LW* 43:115-38.

49. Luther's perceptions of injustice were limited by a number of contextual factors including (1) his anti-Semitic, Constantinian, and patriarchal worldview; (2) his conflating the orders of society with the orders of creation; and (3) the nonexistence, in the pre-modern conceptual world, of the concept of organized social structural change. These factors—among others—led Luther to assume a divinely ordained social hierarchy and to align himself with the political powers that enforced it and embraced the new theology. Thus, in some arenas, Luther was aligned with injustice which he failed to challenge, as seen most clearly in his demonizing of Jewish people, and his denunciation of the peasant uprising and of the "radical" reformers.

50. "An Epistle from the LWF Global Consultation on *Diakonia*," 1. For further discussion of Luther's sense of the power for neighbor-love given by God in the "second kind of righteousness" and in the eucharist, see Cynthia Moe-Lobeda, *Healing a Broken World: Globalization and God* (Minneapolis: Fortress, 2002), chapters 4 and 5.

51. Speaking of the "free public market," Luther writes, "Daily the poor are defrauded. New burdens and high prices are imposed. Everyone misuses the market in his own willful, conceited, arrogant way, as if it were

his right and privilege to sell his goods as dearly as he pleases without a word of criticism." Luther's comments on the tenth commandment in the Large Catechism. See also, Luther, "Admonition to the Clergy that They Preach against Usury," *Weimar Ausgabe* 51.367, cited in Ulrich Duchrow, *Alternatives to Global Capitalism* (Utrecht: International Books, 1995), 220-21.

52. Luther in fact argued that economic activity should be subject to political constraints. "Selling ought not be an act that is entirely within your own power and discretion, without law or limit." Civil authorities ought establish "rules and regulations," including "ceilings" on prices, he insisted. Luther, "Trade and Usury," *Luther's Works* 45: 249-50.

53. Martin Luther, "Trade and Usury," 261, 247-51. See also the entirety of "Trade and Usury," (*LW* 45: 244-308) and Luther's comments on the first, fifth, sixth, seventh, and ninth/tenth commandments and on the fourth petition of the Lord's Prayer in the Large Catechism.

54. Chicago: ELCA, 1990.

55. "Vision and Expectations," 15.

56. *Constitutions,* 16.11.F91.a.8.

57. Ibid., 16.11.E97.

58. Oppression may be said to have five faces: marginalization, domination, violence, powerlessness, and cultural imperialism. See Iris Marion Young, *Justice and the Politics of Difference* (Princeton: Princeton University Press, 1990).

59. In fact he distinguished two broad categories: particular or legal justice and general justice. The latter consisted of both commutative and distributive justice.

60. In addition, "putative justice"—pertaining to the apprehension, trial, conviction, and punishment of wrongdoers may be seen as a form of legal justice.

61. Richard B. McBrien, "Social Justice: Its in Our Bones." unpublished address cited by Ann Patrick, *Liberating Conscience* (New York: Continuum, 1997), 99.

62. Russell B. Connors and Patrick T. McCormick, *Character, Choices, and Community: The Three Faces of Christian Ethics* (New York: Paulist Press, 1998), 66-67.

63. With the profound impact of Christian realism on political life of the US, and in the context of the sharp split between public and private realms of life, justice tends to be seen as the moral norm of public life and love the moral norm of private life. As noted in chapter 1, the dangers of this distinction are profound.

64. This tension is described and analyzed well by Robert A. Dahl in *Democracy and its Critics* (New Haven: Yale University Press, 1989).

65. That shift is in itself suspect if a distributive notion of justice, precludes other dimensions of justice. See Iris Marion Young, *Justice and the Politics of Difference* (Princeton: Princeton University Press, 1990), 33-40.

66. See, for example, Karen Lebacqz, *Justice in an Unjust World: Foundations for a Christian Approach to Justice* (Minneapolis: Augsburg, 1987).

67. "The Reconstruction of the Social Order" *(Quadragesimo Anno)*, Encyclical of Pope Pius XI, 1931.

68. This book refers to what has been known as the *Old Testament* as the *Hebrew Bible*, a move now very common in both church circles and academic theological circles.

69. Bruce C. Birch, *Let Justice Roll Down: The Old Testament, Ethics, and Christian Life* (Louisville: Westminster/John Knox, 1991), 154.

70. Ibid., 155.

71. Ibid.

72. Ibid., 261.

73. Karen Bloomquist, "Seeking Justice," *Between Vision and Reality: Lutheran Churches in Transition*, LWF Documentation 47 (Geneva: LWF, 2001), 253.

74. "Visions and Expectations," 15.

75. "Visions and Expectations," 15.

76. These are verbs used in citations already made in this book, from "Visions and Expectations" (the first two), *Constitution*, Order of Baptism in the *LBW*, and *Constitution*, respectively.

77. Constitution, 7:31:12.

78. LWF, *Between Vision and Reality*, 26.

79. "An Epistle from the LWF Global Consultation on *Diakonia*," 1.

80. Luther distinguishes between two kinds of knowledge of God. The first is general knowledge, which all people have through natural reason, available through philosophy, as well as through creation in which God is present. This kind of knowledge reveals the invisible things of God—the attributes of God such as goodness, wisdom, etc. It is limited in two crucial ways: it doesn't know that God is *pro nobis* (for us), and knows only *that* God is and God's attributes, but does not know *who* God is. The other kind of knowledge is hidden in the suffering and crucified Christ—in the cross. In the "Heidelberg Disputation," Luther explains that this is the true knowledge of God that leads to salvation. Paul Althaus, in *The Theology of Martin Luther* (Philadelphia: Fortress Press, 1966), 28, explains that when Luther says that "God is known only in suffering," he means both Christ's and human beings' suffering.

81. See, for example, Martin Luther, "Whether One May Flee from a Deadly Plague," 115-38.

82. See chapters 4 and 5.

83. "The Use of the Means of Grace," Principle 14.

84. Dietrich Bonhoeffer, *Sanctorum Communio*, trans. R.H. Fuller (New York: Macmillan, 1963), in Bonhoeffer, *A Testament to Freedom*, ed. Geffrey B. Kelly and F. Burton Nelson (San Francisco: HarperCollins, 1990, 1995), 57.

85. At the 2003 Lutheran World Federation Assembly, the organization's name was changed from "The Lutheran World Federation" to "The Lutheran World Federation—A Communion of Churches."

86. This move followed a great deal of study and deliberation.

87. William Lesher, "An Invitation to a Global Table Talk," in Mark Thomsen and Vitor Westhelle, eds., *Envisioning a Lutheran Communion: Perspectives for the Twenty-first Century* (Minneapolis: Kirk House, 2002).

88. "For the Healing of the World," is the title of the most recent (2003) LWF assembly.

89. Dietrich Bonhoeffer, *Letters and Papers from Prison*, ed. Eberhard Bethge (New York: Macmillan, 1971), 17.

90. Tore Johnson, Church of Norway, a delegate to the 2003 Lutheran

World Federation Assembly, addressing the assembly in a plenary session.

91. For an excellent brief summary of three broad phases in the history of the LWF as those phases related to shifts in the meaning, central task, method, and subject of theology, see Vitor Westhelle, "And the Walls Come Tumbling Down: Globalization and Fragmentation in the LWF," *Dialog* 36:1 (Winter 1997).

92. "Ten Theses on the Role of Theology in the LWF," in "Proceedings," LWF Program Committee for Theology and Studies, Exhibit 3, pp. 2-3, cited in LWF *Between Vision and Reality*, 497-8.

93. "Ecumenism: The Vision of the Evangelical Lutheran Church in America," 1991, 1.

94. Martin Luther, "Sermon on 16th Sunday after Trinity," in Lenker 8: 267.

95. Martin Luther in Lenker 8: 277.

96. Martin Luther in Lenker 8: 280.

Chapter 3

1. "Faithful Yet Changing," third strategic direction.

2. Some within the church argue that neighbor-love extends also to other-than-human-kind. With qualifications, I agree, but that is not the issue at this particular point in this inquiry.

3. To preach, in Luther's understanding, was to speak the living Christ.

4. Martin Luther, "Lectures on Romans," *LW* 25:260.

5. Regarding the "second kind of righteousness," see the section of this book titled "To Serve All People, Following the Example of Our Lord Jesus . . ." Regarding Word and Eucharist, see the section called "To Hear the Word of God and Share in the Lord's Supper."

6. Bishop Bernardino Mandlate, in a presentation to the United Nations PrepCom for the World Summit for Social Development Plus Ten, New York, February 1999.

7. Author's conversation with a Mexican woman, met while leading a delegation of North American public-elected officials on a study tour in Mexico and Central America.

8. Martin Luther, "The Blessed Sacrament of the Holy and True Body and Blood of Christ, and the Brotherhoods," in Lull, 260.

9. Martin Luther, *WA* 2.413.27, cited by Forell, *Faith Active in Love,* 92.

10. Martin Luther, "Third Sermon for Pentecost Sunday," in Lenker, 3:321.

11. "Vision and Expectations," 15.

12. Prominent recent theological voices have suggested that while "guilt and condemnation" was the form of anxiety characterizing human existence in the medieval and Reformation West, it is not the defining anxiety of the modern era. Tillich, for example, insisted that "meaninglessness and despair" have, in the modern era, replaced the "guilt and condemnation" that Luther addressed. The 2000 Campbell Seminary, hosted by Columbia Theological Seminary, called together representatives of the church ecumenical from four continents to contemplate the mission of the church in the 21st century. Their conclusion, elaborated in *Hope for the World: Mission in a Global Context,* ed. Walter Brueggemann (Louisville: Westminster/John Knox, 2001), is that "at the outset of the third millennium, the spiritual condition of humankind seems one of despair" and that "the mission of the Christian movement in the twenty-first century is to confess hope in action" (14, 15).

13. The faces of despair and powerlessness are, at the very least, three: (1) despair that we can do nothing substantive to thwart the powers of death and destruction at work with a fury in our world today; (2) despair that the power and presence of God is not, in fact, at work to "change and renew the world;" (3) the despair of the dispossessed, that the forces which torment and threaten the lives of their children cannot be stopped.

14. The words are Douglas John Hall's.

15. For a more thorough discussion of moral agency in relationship to the moral norm of neighbor-love, see Moe-Lobeda, *Healing a Broken World,* 35–38.

16. Acquittal by God in a seemingly "legal" form.

17. Luther, "The Sacrament of the Body and Blood of Christ—Against the Fanatics," 331.

18. As cited by Karen Case in *Facing White Blindness: The Vital Role of an Historical Critical Approach to Race for a White Christian Ethics of Liberation* (dissertation, Union Theological Seminary), 1.

Chapter 4
1. Martin Luther, "Prefaces to the New Testament," *LW* 35:370.
2. Martin Luther, "Sermons on the Gospel of John," *LW* 23:146.
3. The primary source is the Pauline tradition. See, for example, Rom. 12:4-5, 1 Cor. 12:27, and Eph. 1:22-23 and 5:29-30.
4. Articles VII and VIII. "The Use of the Means of Grace," Principle 14, also equates the church with the "body of Christ."
5. Christopher Morse, *Not Every Spirit: A Dogmatics of Christian Disbelief* (Valley Forge: Trinity Press International, 1994), 288.
6. The writings of Luther upon which I draw most heavily for this understanding of "the indwelling Christ" and the implications for the public church are: "The Freedom of a Christian," "The Blessed Sacrament of the Holy and True Body and Blood of Christ, and the Brotherhoods," "Two Kinds of Righteousness," "Disputation Concerning Justification," "The Heidelberg Disputation," and the sermons cited in this book.
7. Martin Luther, "Third Sermon for Pentecost Sunday," in Lenker, 3:316.
8. Martin Luther, "Sermon on the 16th Sunday after Trinity," in Lenker, 8:279-80.
9. Martin Luther, "Third Sermon for Pentecost Sunday," 317.
10. Ibid., 321.
11. Martin Luther, "The Heidelberg Disputation," in Lull, 47.
12. Martin Luther, "The Blessed Sacrament of the Holy and True Body and Blood of Christ, and the Brotherhoods," in Lull, 251.
13. Martin Luther, "Sermon on the 16th Sunday after Trinity," 279.
14. Martin Luther, "Sermon on the Third Sunday after Epiphany," in Lenker, 2:73-74.
15. Ibid.
16. Stephen Ozment, "Luther and the Late Middle Ages: The Formation of Reformation Thought," in *Transition and Revolution: Problems and Issues of European Renaissance and Reformation History*, ed. Robert M. Kingdom (Minneapolis: Fortress, 1974), 109-29.
17. Ibid., 117–119. Ozment summarizes two versions of the late medieval theology against which Luther argued. The first was formulated by

Aquinas, and the second was adjusted by the Ockhamists—including Gabriel Biel—who wanted to preserve more human freedom. Both versions affirm the necessity and possibility of humans contributing decisively to their own salvation. The "synteresis," a spark of goodness in one's reason that conforms to God, enables union based upon likeness.

18. Bonhoeffer, *Sanctorum Communio,* 56.

19. "The relation between the divine love and human love is wrongly understood if we say that the divine love [is] . . . solely for the purpose of setting human love in motion . . . On the contrary . . . the love with which [humans] love God and neighbor is the love of God and no other . . . [T]here is no love which is free or independent from the love of God." Dietrich Bonhoeffer, *Ethics,* ed. Eberhard Bethge (New York: Simon and Schuster, 1995), 55-56.

20. This sense of the form of Christ taking form in and among the faithful is expressed most explicitly by Bonhoeffer in elaborating the third approach to ethics, "conformation with the form of Christ," seen in his *Ethics,* ch. III, esp. 81–89. There he writes, for example: "The Church is nothing but a section of humanity in which Christ has really taken form" (85). The church is "the place where Jesus Christ's taking form is proclaimed and accomplished" (89). Throughout Bonhoeffer's work, the process of "conformation with the form of Christ" entails obedience to the will of God and responsibility in the world. In the last year of his life (perhaps even from the time just before his imprisonment, when "Ten Years After"—located in *Letters and Papers from Prison* [New York: Collier Books, 1972]—and the last "approach" in *Ethics* were written), the nature of "conformation with the form of Christ" develops from active proclamation to a form of faithfulness in a season of silence. It is a form largely unknown, but characterized by silence, waiting, and preparation for the time when once again the redeeming, renewing Word may be proclaimed. The language of "Christ dwelling in" is present also in Bonhoeffer's *Cost of Discipleship* (New York: Simon and Schuster, 1995), 303, although that work is not our primary source here.

21. Martin Luther, *LW,* 26, as cited by Larry Rasmussen, "Luther and a Gospel of Earth," *Union Seminary Quarterly Review* 51, no. 1–2 (1997), 22.

22. *LBW,* 123.

23. Martin Luther, "Sermon on the 16th Sunday after Trinity," 275.

24. Ibid.

25. Martin Luther, "Third Sermon for Pentecost Sunday," 316-317.

26. Ibid.

27. Martin Luther, "Freedom of a Christian," in Lull, 619.

28. "Faithful Yet Changing," mission statement, first statement of vision.

29. Martin Luther, "That These Words of Christ, 'This is My Body,' etc., Still Stand Firm against the Fanatics," *LW* 37:58.

30. Martin Luther, "Confession Concerning Christ's Supper," in Lull, 397.

31. Ibid., 387.

32. Ibid., 386.

33. Martin Luther, "The Sacrament of the Body and Blood of Christ— Against the Fanatics," 321.

34. As Mary Solberg points out in her *Compelling Knowledge,* "[F]or Luther . . . the proper subject of theology is the divine-human relationship . . ." (98).

35. See Larry Rasmussen with Cynthia Moe-Lobeda, "The Reform Dynamic," in *The Promise of Lutheran Ethics,* ed. Karen Bloomquist and John Stumme (Minneapolis: Fortress Press, 1998).

36. Martin Luther, "Sacrament of the Body and Blood of Christ—Against the Fanatics," 321.

37. *Constitutions,* 16.11.E97.

38. *LBW,* 68.

39. Martin Luther, *LW* 26, as cited by Larry Rasmussen, "Luther and a Gospel of Earth," 22.

40. Martin Luther, *WA* 23.134.34, as cited by Larry Rasmussen, "Luther and a Gospel of Earth," 22, citing Paul Santmire, *The Travail of Nature: The Ambiguous Ecological Promise of Christian Theology* (Philadelphia: Fortress Press, 1985), 129.

41. Martin Luther, "That These Words of Christ, 'This is My Body,'" 58.

42. Martin Luther, "The Sacrament of the Body and Blood of Christ— Against the Fanatics," 321.

43. Thomas Berry, *The Great Work* (New York: Bell Tower, 1999).

44. United Nations Development Programme, *Human Development Report 1998* (New York: Oxford University Press, 1998), 29-30.
45. Author's conversation with Jesuit priest Jon Sobrino, in San Salvador, while leading a delegation of North Americans on a study tour in Mexico and Central America.
46. http://*www.formal.stanford.edu/jmc/progress/ucs-statement.txt*.
47. The language in this sentence draws upon words of Larry Rasmussen.
48. For an excellent and highly readable discussion of Luther's theology of the cross, see Solberg, *Compelling Knowledge*.
49. "The way" is a central motif of discipleship in Mark.
50. In first-century Palestine, the cross was an instrument for executing rebels against the Roman Empire.
51. "An Epistle from the LWF Global Consultation on *Diakonia*," 2.
52. "Faithful Yet Changing," mission statement.
53. Martin Luther, *LW*, 26, as cited by Larry Rasmussen, "Luther and a Gospel of Earth," 22.

Chapter 5

1. Martin Luther, "The Large Catechism (1529)," in Theodore G. Tappert, ed. and trans., *The Book of Concord: Confessions of the Evangelical Lutheran Church* (Philadelphia: Fortress, 1959), 368.
2. This distinction is made clear in the Spanish language. Two Spanish words translate the English "to know." One, "*saber*," refers to cognitive knowledge of something. The other, "*conocer*," refers to knowing as being in relationship with.
3. The term solidarity is overused and misused. The many problems with it are not easily seen from eyes of privilege. Yet, I continue to use the norm of solidarity, because to lose it would be a great loss. Problems with this concept and responses to them are sketched in Moe-Lobeda, *Healing a Broken World*, 118-223.
4. Walter Brueggemann, "Voices of the Night—Against Justice," 17.
5. Dietrich Bonhoeffer, *Letters and Papers from Prison*, 17.
6. For example, many ELCA congregations have sister congregations among more vulnerable people; our bishops have traveled to Central America, Africa, and the Middle East, listening especially to those who

are suffering; the voices, faith, hopes, and prayers of neighbors on the margins of power are welcomed in song and art; our human service agencies include, as members of their boards and advisory councils, people of limited options and special needs served by the agencies.

7. Emilie M. Townes, *Breaking the Fine Rain of Death* (New York: Continuum, 2001), 12.

8. Townes, 24, drawing upon the ideas of Walter Brueggemann, "The Costly Loss of Lament," *Journal for the Study of the Old Testament* 36 (1986): 60.

9. Ibid.

10. Ibid.

11. *LBW,* 123.

12. Meeks, 17.

Closing

1. *Constitutions,* 4.01–02.

2. "Faithful Yet Changing," mission statement.

OTHER BOOKS FROM THE
LUTHERAN VOICES SERIES

Will I Sing Again? by John McCullough Bade
96 pages, 0-8066-4998-4

Author John McCullough Bade reflects on his personal
struggle with Parkinson's Disease, expressing his journey in startling poetry and prose.

Getting Ready for the New Life by Richard Bansemer
96 pages, 0-8066-4988-7

Author Richard Bansemer provides comfort and
encouragement for those facing illness and death, and
for those who care for them, through Scriptural texts,
reflections, and prayers.

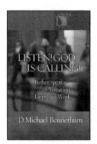

Listen! God Is Calling by D. Michael Bennethum
96 pages, 0-8066-4991-7

Author D. Michael Bennethum presents Martin
Luther's teaching on vocation as a resource both for
individual believers and for congregations. Bennethum
guides readers to listen for God's call in every aspect of
life.

On a Wing and a Prayer by Michael L. Cooper-White
96 pages, 0-8066-4992-5

Author Michael L. Cooper-White uses the language of
aviation to look at the principles of leadership and
apply them to congregations and other organizations.

Let the Servant Church Arise!
by Barbara DeGrote-Sorensen
and David Allen Sorensen
96 pages, 0-8066-4995-X

Authors Barbara DeGrote-Sorensen and David Allen
Sorensen explore all aspects of Christian servanthood
and how it can have a profound effect on both church
and civil communities.

Our Lives Are Not Our Own
by Rochelle Melander and Harold Eppley
96 pages, 0-8066-4999-2

Authors Rochelle Melander and Harold Eppley
encourage personal reflective and creative dialogue
about Christian accountability for the use of our lives,
possessions, and abilities.

Reclaiming the "L" Word by Kelly A. Fryer
112 pages, 0-8066-4596-2

Inspirational, engaging, and challenging, author Kelly
A. Fryer sets forth five Guiding Principles to ignite the
church in a book that is a must-read for pastors and
congregational leaders!

Other Books from the
Lutheran Voices Series

Water from the Rock by Ann E. Hafften
96 pages, 0-8066-4989-5

Contributing editor Ann E. Hafften provides articles,
commentary, and stories from prominent Lutherans
living in the strife-torn land of Palestine.

Who Do You Say That I Am? by Susan K. Hedahl
96 pages, 0-8066-4990-9

Author Susan K. Hedahl provides some basic defini-
tions of preaching in the post-modern age and invites
readers into a Holy encounter with Jesus through
Lutheran preaching.

Signs of Belonging by Mary E. Hinkle
96 pages, 0-8066-4997-6

Author Mary E. Hinkle explores Luther's teaching on
the seven marks of the church, drawing the reader into
a personal, spiritual exploration in dialogue with biblical wisdom.

Speaking of Trust by Martin E. Marty
160 pages, 0-8066-4994-1

Author Martin E. Marty brings together passages from Luther's preaching on the Sermon on the Mount and his own comments about the place of trust in the life of faith.

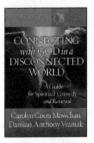

Connecting with God in a Disconnected World
by Carolyn Coon Mowchan
and Damian Anthony Vraniak.
96 pages, 0-8066-4996-8

Authors Carolyn Coon Mowchan and Damian Anthony Vraniak encourage adult readers to examine the barriers that keep us from experiencing a more full relationship with God.

Give Us This Day by Craig L. Nessan
96 pages, 0-8066-4993-3

Author Craig L. Nessan summons the Christian church to listen to the cries of the hungry and commit itself to ending hunger as a matter of *status confessionis*.

OTHER RESOURCES FROM
AUGSBURG FORTRESS, PUBLISHERS

Healing a Broken World
by Cynthia D. Moe-Lobeda
242 pages, 0-8006-3250-8

Author Cynthia D. Moe-Lobeda makes clear that economic globalization is something Christians must resist and finds the strength and courage to resist this force through the unification of spirituality and ethics.

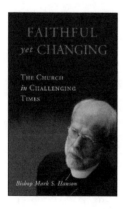

Faithful Yet Changing
by Bishop Mark S. Hanson
82 pages, 0-8066-4474-5

Author Bishop Mark S. Hanson sets forth a vision for the church—a church faithful to the Scriptures and its tradition, yet changing to meet the new challenges of our diverse, fragmented world.